ESCAPE THE COMING NIGHT

DR. DAVID JEREMIAH
WITH C.C. CARLSON

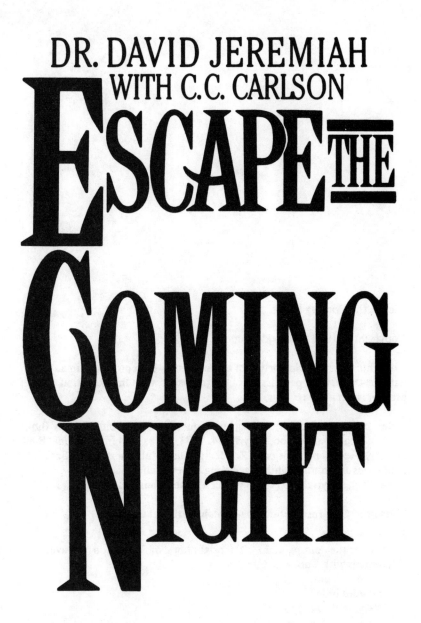

ESCAPE THE COMING NIGHT

WORD PUBLISHING
Dallas·London·Vancouver·Melbourne

Escape the Coming Night

Copyright © 1990 by David Jeremiah

Unless otherwise indicated all Scripture quotations are from the Holy Bible, New International Version, copyright © 1973, 1978, 1984 International Bible Society. Used by permission of Zondervan Bible Publishers. Other Scripture quotations are from the authorized King James Version (KJV), and *The Living Bible* (TLB), copyright 1971 by Tyndale House Publishers, Wheaton, IL.

Library of Congress Cataloging-in-Publication Data

Jeremiah, David.
    Escape the coming night : the bright hope of Revelation / David Jeremiah with Carole C. Carlson.
        p.   cm.
    Includes index.
    ISBN 0-8499-3295-5
    1. Bible. N.T. Revelation—Commentaries.   I. Carlson, Carole C. II. Title.
    BS2825.3.J46   1991
    228'.06—dc20   90-49409
                                                                         CIP

Printed in the United States of America

4 5 6 7 8 9 LBM 17 16 15 14 13

"But you, brothers, are not in darkness so that this day should surprise you like a thief. . . . *We do not belong to the night* or to the darkness. . . . let us not be like others who are asleep, but let us be alert . . ."

(1 Thessalonians 5:4–6, emphasis added).

CONTENTS

INTRODUCTION

When we started this book the Berlin wall was standing and the cold war was continuing its forty-year chill. Overnight that seemed to change, as we watched the Iron Curtain fray and the capitals of the nations rejoice in new hope for a free world.

However, just when we began to feel the pressure lift from our tension-laden minds, a new tyranny invades the scene. It may be a world leader, wielding a threat of chemical warfare, or maniacal gunmen spraying death and injury on innocent children. It may be an economic crisis or an international scandal that shatters our temporary calm.

If we have learned anything from the past few years, it has been this . . . peace is fragile.

How long will God allow the earth and its inhabitants to destroy themselves before He intervenes? This is the question many are asking, whether they believe in a personal God or not. I do not know the answer, nor does anyone else. But what I do know is that today, more than any other time in the history of man, events are occurring that foreshadow things to come.

The alignment of nations, the collapse of ethical and moral values, and the weakening influence of our churches and their leaders are some of the indicators of the era directly preceding the return of Christ.

I believe there is one sure word of truth and that is the Bible. As I studied the awesome events recorded in Revelation, I felt a sense of urgency to attempt to unravel their imagery and explain their significance. From the sometimes unfathomable chapters of the last book in the Bible comes some astonishing information about the end of this world as we know it.

Within these pages are the hope and encouragement we need to lift us from the gray gloom of present events to the promise of a brilliant future.

Many scholars have written commentaries on the Book of Revelation, and I do not pretend to write something which only a Bible student or seminary graduate can comprehend. This book is intended for the person who has never read Revelation, because it didn't make sense to him, or to the person who has read it and it still didn't make sense.

There are differences of opinion on some theological points, and I expect some of my ideas may cause controversy. However, I have tried to be a careful conservative in scholarship without being pedantic in style.

Night is coming . . . a darkness that will cover this globe in suffering and sorrow such as we have never known. But we must not sit and wring our hands about the state of the world. God has provided a way to escape the coming night. Now is the time to tell everyone about the hope of a brand new world waiting for us. This book is about that hope.

DAVID JEREMIAH

Part I

REVELATION:
KEY TO THE FUTURE

1

MOUNTAIN WARNINGS

Old Harry was a stubborn man who had become a legend in the Pacific Northwest. Though he was warned repeatedly that his life was in jeopardy, he just laughed.

Red flags and danger signs are often ignored. Take Harry, for instance. His story is a harbinger for us—for today, this decade, and the new millennium.

He lived at the foot of a quiet mountain—at least she had been quiet for 123 years. Sometimes she stirred to spit cinder ash or drool lava from her cavernous crater. Occasionally she looked down steep snowfields and rumbled a muted threat to the people who explored the lush forests and mountain meadows below. Some thought Bigfoot, the legendary giant beast, stalked her slopes.

But Mt. St. Helens was seething inside, ready to unleash her force upon unbelieving admirers. She was awesome and mysterious, but only threatening to the few who understood her power.

March 1980, an earthquake registering 4.1 on the Richter

Scale was reported near Mt. St. Helens in southwestern Washington state. Forest rangers were advised of possible dangers from avalanches which could trap skiers or climbers. Most folks were unconcerned. The mountain setting was tranquil as people anticipated spring, a time for renewal. The earth was singing with new warmth.

On March 27, a ranger heard what he thought was a sonic boom. The mountain had erupted!

Scientists rushed to assess the explosive potential of the mountain; they painted a frightening scenario of future destruction. People listened, but many could not comprehend a disaster of such magnitude.

Old Harry probably read the news stories while he ate a solitary breakfast and fed scraps to his sixteen cats. "Nobody knows more about this mountain than Harry and it don't dare blow up on him," he bragged.

Days and weeks passed and some became impatient with the geologists' negative reports. "People would lose their concern of anything ever happening and wanted to get back to business as usual. Everybody kind of heard the geologists say what they wanted to hear them say. They weren't really listening to them"[1]

When sheriff's deputies ordered all residents on the shores of Spirit Lake, at the base of the mountain, to leave for safety, Harry said, "I'm havin' a hell of a time livin' my life alone. I'm king of all I survey, I got plenty of whiskey, I got food enough for fifteen years, and I'm settin' high on the hog."[2]

Sunday morning, May 18, 1980, the mountain exploded and hurled pulverized rock and ash almost fourteen miles high. The force of the blast flattened trees, uprooting and smashing them like millions of dominoes spreading out from the crater. Steam, ash, and gases spouted from the incinerated vegetation, mud flows flooded the rivers and transformed the beautiful mountain lands into a ghastly charred landscape.

The mountain's vengeance was 500 times greater than the nuclear bomb which leveled Hiroshima.

The warnings were over. There was no longer any time to run.

Will We Listen?

In the 1990s there is a great stirring around the world. The high-decibel threats of communism are quieting as governments topple and new leaders emerge. Many oppressed people are feeling a freedom they have never known.

Time magazine had a cover story showing the heads of the world's two most powerful countries smiling at each other over the words, "Building a New World."

We begin to rejoice that old animosities are dissolving and experience new hope for peace in the the world community, but at the same time suspect that we are being lulled into a false security.

Warnings have been posted about dangers in the road ahead. We can either watch and listen or ignore the signs.

The signs of the time are on a fast track, pointing to the final days of Bible prophecy that have been recorded for almost 2,000 years. It's true that many people shrug their shoulders and say, "Is this like the guy who said the end of the world would come on September 16, 1988? Come on now! I've heard this stuff before."

The apostle Peter said: "First, I want to remind you that in the last days there will come scoffers who will do every wrong they can think of, and laugh at the truth. This will be their line of argument: 'So Jesus promised to come back, did he? Then where is he? He'll never come! Why, as far back as anyone can remember everything has remained exactly as it was since the first day of creation'" (2 Peter 3:3, 4 TLB).

There is a book in the Bible which scoffers should read. It contains warnings far more solemn than those directed at

Harry. The book of Revelation predicts the climax of the ages and the sequence of events leading up to the return of Jesus Christ. Furthermore, this book explains where every person will be for all eternity.

Who Can Predict the Future?

When someone asks me, "When is your birthday?" I become wary. I don't believe they plan to send me a present. They probably want to know what sign I live under so they can tell me how to run my life. In spite of the nonsense of astrological predictions, most of the major newspapers in the country continue to carry these columns, and many people will use these silly predictions to determine how they will plan their daily activities and future goals. Even people who are prominent in public life consult astrologers and psychics, searching for answers to life's complexities.

God predicts the future with inerrant accuracy. He knows the end from the beginning. However, He gives us the guide for the present. "Therefore do not worry about tomorrow, for tomorrow will worry about itself. Each day has enough trouble of its own" (Matthew 6:34).

We are not to worry about tomorrow, but He wants us to understand the future so we will know how to live *today.* His Book is filled with predictions which have already been fulfilled. Look at just a few of them.

True to Date

In the Old Testament there are more than 300 references to the coming Messiah that were fulfilled in Jesus Christ. In Genesis 3:15 we find the first reference to the fact that the Savior of the world would be born of "the seed of the woman" (KJV). This ancient promise predicts a struggle between Israel's Messiah and Satan, and foretells the Messiah's eventual victory.

The prophet Isaiah tells that the Messiah will be born of a virgin. It was prophesied that He would be the Son of God, and He would trace His humanity to Abraham, father of the Jewish nation. He would come from the tribe of Judah and the house of David. Micah foretold that He would be born in Bethlehem and the psalmist wrote that He shall be called Lord.[3]

It was predicted that the coming Messiah would be a prophet, a judge, and a king. This Man whom the Jews were waiting for (and many are still seeking) would be more than an ordinary human being, for the Spirit of the Lord would give Him wisdom and knowledge beyond our comprehension.[4]

To me, prophecy is the most absorbing study in the Bible. The coming Messiah's ministry was described in such detail that no other person could have fulfilled the description.

The Perfect Résumé

Imagine a twentieth-century executive recruiter listing these requirements for a chief executive officer:

An unqualified recommendation by a community leader (John the Baptist).

His term of office to begin in Galilee.

He must perform miracles.

He must teach his management team by using illustrations.

He should expose dishonest members of the firm and fire them.

He must bring a new era of understanding and wisdom to a faltering company.

From all of the applicants, one man alone steps out of history and says, "I'm your man." He fills every requirement so perfectly that the search team would be overwhelmed.

Some Old Testament prophets were instructed to give doleful predictions. More than 700 years before the birth of Christ, Isaiah said that He would be despised, wounded, bruised, and oppressed (53:3, 5, 7). The same old prophet said He would be crucified with thieves and rejected by His own people.

When we see the prophecies fulfilled in the life of Jesus, how can we doubt that He was the Messiah, the Christ, the Son of God? The cruel manner in which He would die, the grave where He would be buried, and His glorious resurrection were predicted by holy men, led by God to write His inspired Word.

After Jesus was resurrected, He appeared to His disciples over a period of forty days, and told them many things. They must have listened with an intensity they had never experienced before, with a new urgency in their questions: "When will you establish the kingdom of Israel, Lord?" Jesus told them, as He had before, that they were not to know the time of His return and the establishment of His kingdom, but to watch for the signs of the times. As they were pondering this answer, He suddenly was lifted out of sight and disappeared into a cloud.

While the apostles stood with their mouths open, two men in white clothing came and gave the first post-Christian prophetic message:

"'Men of Galilee,' they said, 'why do you stand here looking into the sky? This same Jesus, who has been taken from you into heaven, will come back in the same way you have seen him go into heaven'" (Acts 1:11).

When He left earth He was only in His thirties. Yet no other man in history has ever made such an impact on this planet.

He is coming again. More than 300 times in the New Testament and one entire, exciting book describes in detail the time and chronological events leading up to His return.

The Author with the Key

The book that tells us the awesome events which will bring history to a finale is sometimes called "The Revelation of St. John the Divine," or "The Revelation of John." The correct title should be "The Revelation of Jesus Christ." John did not write an imaginative piece of spiritual fiction; he was chosen by Jesus to record the epic which would forever change the lives of those who read and understand it.

John, "the disciple whom Jesus loved," was special to Jesus. It wasn't that Jesus didn't love His other disciples, but there was a particular bond with this one. John and his brother, James, were called "Sons of Thunder" when they were young, but as he grew older, John became known for his gentleness; the thunder became a distant rumble.

John was bold, however, in telling everyone about Jesus. That severely offended Domitian, the Emperor of Rome from A.D. 81–96. This pompous fellow had assumed the title "Master and god," and he demanded that people take an oath to worship him. The apostle John refused to obey such a command, and for this crime he was sent to the isolated island of Patmos, a rocky, almost treeless wasteland, covered with volcanic hills and dented with caves. Domitian must have thought an old man like John, who was now in his nineties, could not survive long in such cruel exile.

Hovering in a barren grotto with criminals of every stripe, John probably approached his banishment as an opportunity to reach those wretched people with the love of Christ. However, he was given a greater mission; God told him of future events which would change the course of the world forever.

God sent an angel to communicate with John, and John tells us:

"The revelation of Jesus Christ, which God gave him *to show his servants what must soon take place.* He made it known by sending his angel to his servant John, who testifies to everything he saw—that is, the word of God and the testimony of Jesus Christ" (Revelation 1:1, 2, emphasis added).

No Longer a Mystery

The word "revelation" means the disclosure of that which was previously hidden or unknown. The book of Revelation tells us that Jesus is coming again, how He is coming, and what condition the world will be in when He comes.

People frequently ask, "Why must Jesus come again?" The reasons are evident in the two phases of His return.

First, Jesus must return again to take His church to be with Him forever. The church is called the bride of Christ, and just as a bride eagerly awaits the day she will be united with the one she loves, so the church, made up of believers in Jesus, waits to be united with the Bridegroom. In heaven there will be the Marriage Supper of the Lamb, the symbolic joining of Christ, the Bridegroom, with the church as the bride, to be one forever in eternity.

Phase One in the second coming of Christ is called the Rapture. This is the great magnet process, when all true believers in Jesus Christ, sensitized to Him, will be drawn like a magnet to be with Him (1 Thessalonians 4:17).

Phase Two will take place at the end of a seven-year period after the Rapture, when Christ returns to reign over His earthly kingdom.

When Christ takes His own to heaven (those whose earthly bodies have died and those who are alive at that time), they will stand before the judgment seat of Christ. Some people have asked, "If there are so many to be judged, why doesn't Christ judge them immediately on their death, instead of letting all those millions of people pile up at the last minute?"

The answer is that we don't finish our work when we die. It lives on after us. What we have done on earth, if it amounts to anything, continues after we die physically. How could there be awards and judgments when our earthly life is over? Our influence upon friends, family, the people we knew during our lifetimes, does not cease when our obituaries appear in the local paper.

I know of Kristin, a fourteen-year-old girl who died after a lingering and painful bout with cancer. One of her last concerns was for her friends who did not know Jesus Christ as she did. She asked her mother, "Who will tell them about Jesus after I'm gone?" Her testimony will live on and its ripple effect will touch more lives than we will ever know until the kingdom comes.

Many people are still piling up points before appearing at the judgment seat in heaven. For instance, D. L. Moody went to be with the Lord in 1899, but his influence and the school he founded, Moody Bible Institute, have continued for decades.

What on Earth Is Happening

While Christians are appearing for their awards, the people remaining on earth will be living in the worst time of final history. Although the book of Revelation describes this time called the Tribulation, some of the great Christians of the past, like Martin Luther and John Calvin, virtually ignored this last book in the Bible. Perhaps they thought that some of the signs preceding the Second Coming were so obscure in their time that Revelation was a vast mystery to them. Now it is being understood and unraveled faster than the last pages of an Agatha Christie novel.

Christ will return not only to reward His own, but to judge the world. Between His first appearance and His second will be a time of trouble, and then will occur the judgment of all those who rejected Him. This will not be a judgment for believers, for they have already stood before the judgment seat. This will be a judgment with no parole, no lenient sentence, and no pleas of insanity.

Jesus will return for His church, then to judge the world, and finally to rule the world. More than five centuries before

Christ was born, the Jewish prophet Daniel described this scene:

"He was given authority, glory and sovereign power; all peoples, nations and men of every language worshiped him. His dominion is an everlasting dominion that will not pass away, and his kingdom is one that will never be destroyed" (Daniel 7:14).

When Jesus was on earth the first time He didn't rule over a small country. He wasn't mayor of a city, governor of a state, or president of Palestine. But someday His kingdom will encompass not only the world, but the entire universe.

His disciples wanted to know what would be the sign of His coming and the end of the age (Matthew 24:3). Ever since that time people have been asking the same questions. The signs Jesus gave always pointed to establishing His kingdom on earth, not to the Rapture. But coming events cast their shadow before them, and these shadows are gathering around us now. Prophecy is not intended as a mental exercise for believers who are concerned about the intricacies of the Bible. God gives us prophecy so that we can learn how to live.

What Can We Learn from Prophecy?

Revelation reveals the sequence and magnitude of the future, but the New Testament tells us how prophecy can be a dynamic school for self-improvement. Here are a few courses offered:

Problem-Solving. I don't know of a university that offers this course, but the Bible says that understanding the future will put our everyday problems into better perspective (Colossians 3:2).

Advanced Loving. We will be more loving people, because our love will "increase and overflow for each other and for everyone else" as the impact of His coming soon penetrates our beings (1 Thessalonians 3:12, 13).

Church Growth. There's not a pastor of a large or small

church who wouldn't be interested in this course. The best place to be as that important day approaches is in church worshiping or in the world serving (Hebrews 10:25).

Goal-Setting. If we really believed He would come back today, we would change many of our habits. "Dear friends, now we are children of God, and what we will be has not yet been made known. But we know that when he appears, we shall be like him, for we shall see him as he is. Everyone who has this hope in him purifies himself, just as he is pure" (1 John 3:2, 3).

Cheerleading. In the big games, the cheerleaders encourage the crowd. How about a course in encouragement? After Paul had written to the church at Thessalonica and the last events on the time chart had become clearer, he said to those believers, "encourage each other" (1 Thessalonians 4:18). We do not need to be doomsayers, but cheerleaders.

Life-Saving. Even those who can't swim can take this course, for it is the most important one to be offered. Prophecy provides us an urgency to reach others for Jesus Christ, to "snatch others from the fire and save them" (Jude 23).

Rangers for Revelation

When Mt. St. Helens was about to erupt, the forest rangers sounded the alarm. They issued bulletins, knocked on doors, and shouted warnings. The good news is that many listened and escaped. Unfortunately, old Harry, along with his cats and flowers, was buried under tons of rock and mud.

For us, the escape route has been mapped out for almost 2,000 years. As we approach the Third Millennium many people think time is growing short before Christ returns. In the past twenty years, since Bible prophecy captured the attention of the Jesus generation, history has been in high gear.

Are we listening today to the warnings from the mountain of evidence in front of us? Old Harry showed us the foolishness of not being prepared.

2

THE GREATEST
COVER STORY

The Berlin wall crumbles overnight. What a thrilling sight! In quick succession, old regimes topple throughout Eastern Europe. As our minds raced to comprehend the speed of a changing world, commentators and news pundits were saying that the threat of war was steadily fading.

The Bible says there is a time coming "While people are saying, 'Peace and safety,' destruction will come on them suddenly . . ." (1 Thessalonians 5:3).

A short time ago peoples of the world were not talking of peace and safety; this prophecy would have been hard to believe. But today, as West German Chancellor Kohl said, "The wheel of history is turning faster now."[1]

An angel told the Old Testament prophet Daniel that many prophecies would not be understood until the end times. "Go your way, Daniel, because the words are closed up and sealed until the time of the end. . . . those who are wise will understand" (Daniel 12:9, 10).

In Revelation, prophecies are unsealed and John is given

opposite orders. "Then he told me, 'Do not seal up the words of the prophecy of this book, because the time is near'" (Revelation 22:10).

John was told to get the word out! He was to use every method he could to relay this message to the world.

Jesus told John not only to reveal prophecies, but also the order in which they would take place. "Write, therefore, what you have seen, what is now and what will take place later" (Revelation 1:19).

Some people say they can't understand the book of Revelation. Even Martin Luther wrote, "My spirit cannot adapt itself to the book, and a sufficient reason why I do not esteem it highly is that Christ is neither taught nor recognized in it."[2]

Twelve years later, Luther modified his view, but he never fully accepted the last book in the Bible. When Luther lived, the events described in Revelation did not seem possible, but today we should understand them by reading the newspaper headlines.

Down through the centuries, men have been blessed by reading Revelation. Now we live in an era where understanding is added to blessing.

Blessing from His Story

"The revelation of Jesus Christ, which God gave him to show his servants what must soon take place. He made it known by sending his angel to his servant John, who testifies to everything he saw—that is, the word of God and the testimony of Jesus Christ. Blessed is the one who reads the words of this prophecy, and blessed are those who hear it and take to heart what is written in it, because the time is near" (Revelation 1:1–3). These words comprise the "preface" to the book of Revelation.

"Revelation" is the translation of a word which has been misused to convey fear. It's the Greek word *apokalypsis,* which means "uncovering" or "revealing." Revelation, the apocalypse, is the unveiling of Jesus Christ; it is a book that is both about Him and by Him. This book is not a puzzle; it is a completed picture.

The second prophetic phrase in the preface is the Greek *entachie,* which is translated, "shortly come to pass." It means something that will happen suddenly. This has been a dilemma to generations of people before us. They have read the same prophecy and wondered, *Will these things happen in my lifetime?*

Many Christians thought the Lord would return within the generation that saw Israel reborn as a nation in the land of its forefathers. On May 14, 1948, the State of Israel was established and some notable Bible scholars believed that within forty years (a generation) or so of that time, the Rapture would occur. They based this premise upon the words of Jesus: "I tell you the truth, this generation will certainly not pass away until all these things have happened" (Matthew 24:34). Forty years have come and gone, and He has not returned. This is not to discredit those who believed this interpretation, but I think they missed the point.

What it does mean is that those people who see and experience the events Christ spoke of in Matthew 24 will be part of the generation that will be here when Christ returns to establish His kingdom on earth. As we see these events unfold during the Tribulation, the parallel with the predictions of Jesus will be vividly clear.

The Risk of Ignorance

The book of Revelation is sometimes ignored in Bible studies as not being relevant to our daily lives and problems. Louis Talbot, after whom Talbot Theological Seminary was named, expressed it this way:

"Many people treat the book of Revelation like the priest and Levite treated the man who was beaten and robbed in the story of the Good Samaritan . . . they pass by on the other side. The devil has turned thousands of people away from this portion of God's Word. He does not want anyone to read a book that tells of his being cast out of heaven . . . Nor is he anxious for us to read of the ultimate triumph of his number one enemy, Jesus Christ. The more you study the book of Revelation, the more you understand why Satan fights so hard to keep God's people away from it."[3]

That motivates me to get on with this prophetic discovery. If Satan is against it, I'm for it. If Jesus said I'd be blessed by reading and hearing the words of this book, I'll take Him at His word.

Revelation, the only prophetic book in the New Testament, stands alone as a lighthouse in the churning sea of modern turmoil. Its miracles will only be understood by those who have the ears to hear and the ability by the Spirit of God to discern.

The tragedy today is that not only atheists and agnostics deny the miracles of the Bible, but some so-called Christian preachers and teachers, liberal in their outlook and education, consider many biblical miracles to be allegories and reject the supernatural.

Deciphering the Secret Code

Revelation is a book of symbols, some representing people. In the first chapter, Jesus is seen as a judge with a two-edged sword coming out of his mouth. Later, the Antichrist is presented as a beast; the great religious system is described as Babylon the Great. Another important and repetitive symbol is the use of numbers, not the least of which is the ominous mark of the beast, 666.

Numbers are forms of symbols and the number seven, which is called the perfect number, is used fifty-four times in Revelation. John uses the symbolic seven in many places:

seven churches, seven spirits, seven candlesticks, seven stars, seven lamps, seven seals, seven horns, seven eyes, seven angels, seven trumpets, seven thunders, seven heads, seven crowns, and others. Symbolically, the number seven stands for completeness.

Why is there so much symbolism in the book of Revelation? Do you wonder why it couldn't have been as simple and straightforward as the Gospel of John? Here are some reasons.

To begin with, symbolism is not weakened by time. John was able to draw the great images in God's revelation and write them into an exciting drama; symbols can stand the test of the years, without relating to one particular era or culture.

Symbols also impart values and arouse emotions. How much more graphic it is to speak of "beasts," instead of "dictators." There is more color in referring to "Babylon the Great" than the "world system." If our emotions are not aroused by some of the words used as symbols, we should have our red blood count taken.

Then, too, symbols can be used as a secret code. Just as secret projects are given code names, so the prisoner of Patmos had a spiritual code which was circulated to the churches.

The political climate of this period was not unlike that of the 1940s. A diabolically wicked leader, believing in his own ability to rule his empire and establish himself with god-like powers, realized that these people who called themselves Christians had an allegiance to another God. Whereas Hitler annihilated the Jews, the emperor Domitian set out to abolish the influence of the followers of a man called Jesus. Some Christians were killed; others, like John, were imprisoned for their faith.

The early Christians were looking eagerly for the return of their Master, but sixty years after his death this hope was still unfulfilled. John wanted to encourage those believers, so he wrote letters to the churches, urging them to stand firm, not to waver in their faith. However, he had to disguise this message in such a way that the Roman authorities would not understand it. The Christians could decipher this secret code, but Domitian and his henchmen would be puzzled by it. It would be similar to POWs in our century tapping out codes on cell walls to encourage their fellow prisoners.

Just as this symbolism could be understood by the first-century believers, so it is equally vivid to Christians of every age. We can understand the symbolism in Revelation because each symbol is accompanied by its own interpretation.

The seven stars (1:16) are the seven angels (1:20).

The seven lampstands (1:13) are the seven churches (1:20).

The seven lamps are the sevenfold Spirit of God (5:6).

Throughout Scripture symbols occur as a vehicle for divine revelation, but Revelation contains more symbols than any other book in the Bible.

We don't need to be Bible scholars to be able to decode the messages.

Positive and Negative Motivation

One of my friends has an eight-foot bookshelf filled with modern motivational best-sellers. I asked him if he had ever considered one of the greatest motivational treatises in the world, the book of Revelation. He probably thought I had flipped out, but I hope he reads this book and agrees with its motivational impact.

Revelation is the only book in the Bible that motivates its readers by promising a blessing to those who read and obey it—and a curse to those who tamper with it: "I warn everyone who hears the words of the prophecy of this book: If anyone adds anything to them, God will add to him the plagues described in this book. And if anyone takes words away from this book of prophecy, God will take away from him his share in the tree of life and in the holy city, which are described in this book" (22:18, 19).

That is a sobering thought. It should be considered by all those who do not believe in the inerrancy of the Bible or the accuracy of prophecy. Personally, I like positive motivation better, and Revelation has that. There are seven blessings in the book:

1. *"Blessed is the one who reads the words of this prophecy,* and *blessed are those who hear it* and take to heart what is written in it, because the time is near" (1:3).

2. "Then I heard a voice from heaven say, 'Write: *Blessed are the dead* who die in the Lord from now on.' 'Yes,' says the Spirit, 'they will rest from their labor, for their deeds will follow them'" (14:13).

3. "Behold, I come like a thief! *Blessed is he who stays awake* and keeps his clothes with him, so that he may not go naked and be shamefully exposed" (16:15).

4. "Then the angel said to me, 'Write: *Blessed are those who are invited to the wedding supper of the Lamb!'* And he added, 'These are the true words of God'" (19:9).

5. *"Blessed and holy are those who have part in the first resurrection.* The second death has no power over them, but they will be priests of God and of Christ and will reign with him for a thousand years" (20:6).

6. "Behold, I am coming soon! *Blessed is he who keeps the words of the prophecy* in this book" (22:7)

7. *"Blessed are those who wash their robes,* that they may have the right to the tree of life and may go through the gates into the city" (22:14).

Blessings of His Majesty

Nothing reveals the majesty of this book as does John's reaction to the personal revelation of Jesus. When he saw Him, he fell at His feet in a dead faint. I don't know if anyone ever fainted while bowing to the King and Queen of England, or some other monarch—it's possible. John was so overcome he simply fainted.

Jesus must have smiled as He looked at His beloved disciple. He tenderly put His hand on him and told him not to be afraid.

The Jesus of Revelation is not the humble carpenter or the teacher with worn sandals. He is "His Majesty King Jesus"! He doesn't say that He *will be* King, but that He *is* the ruler of the kings, the King of kings.

He is King of heaven—(Daniel 4:37).
He is King of the Jews—(Matthew 2:2)
He is King of Israel—(John 1:49).
He is King of the ages—(1 Timothy 1:17).
He is King of glory—(Psalm 24:7).
He is King of saints—(Revelation 15:3).
He is King of kings—(Revelation 19:16).

If I didn't know that He was in charge, I would be frightened. As the bizarre murder stories, the accelerating global contamination, the collapsing of personal and moral values blare at us each day, I remind myself of the King.

Today we are concerned about who's in charge of the nations of the world. We believe if the right man is elected, or the wrong one ousted, the world will be better. Granted, these are worthwhile bandages for a wounded globe, but not the cure. The second chapter of Daniel tells us that human governments will topple.

Vernard Eiler said, ". . . 'the kings of the earth' are where the action is, theirs is the clout that makes things happen; theirs are the actions determining the course of history. . . . Contrary to their own inflated opinion, that crew does not hold the reins of history. John's very first notice of the kings of the earth is to proclaim that they have a ruler; they are being ruled."[4]

Some may think God is powerless and evil rulers guide the destiny of this planet. Things are not what they seem! Jesus is Lord.

Purpose of Revelation

Revelation presents the King who is coming again, at a time when "every eye will see him" (1:7). The word most often used to describe the second coming of Christ is *parousia*. This is the Greek term for a coming event which immediately changes the situation.

I'm sure schoolchildren today never throw erasers or spitballs when the teacher leaves the room, but they did when I was in school. When the teacher left the room, a wild eraser fight would erupt. The chalky missiles would spread dust all over the room until she returned. Her entrance would be a *parousia*. Erasers would stop in mid-air and every student would be an instant model of pious behavior.

Christ's return will change the situation on earth. He will "return in the clouds," a familiar description of His appearing. When Moses was given the law on Mt. Sinai, a thick cloud surrounded the mountain. When the worship of the tabernacle was set up in the wilderness, a cloud covered the tent of the congregation. At the transfiguration of Jesus, He and the disciples were overshadowed by a bright cloud. When He ascended to heaven a cloud received Him, and Daniel predicted that the Messiah would come with the "clouds of heaven."[5]

On days when the cumulus clouds form in blue skies, I like to imagine that Jesus will appear and all over the earth unbelieving persons will stare with amazement and shock to see Him descend to earth.

The aim of Revelation is not only to present to us the coming King, but also to tell us the purpose of His kingdom. In America we hear the politicians tell us every four years why we should elect them and what their programs will be if they win office. Revelation is the account of Jesus' campaign for the rulership of the earth. We are clearly told of His relationship to the church, His appointment by the Father to the throne, His crusade against the Satanic forces of evil, and His final victory. There is no need to count votes, for He knows the results.

Campaign to Ban the Book

If we believe the Bible is the inspired Word of God, we should expect opposition. Scholars and skeptics (and they are not always synonymous) will attempt to make us doubt.

A motion picture, *The Last Temptation of Christ*, produced in 1988, aroused so much controversy that the cover story for *Time* magazine was "Who Is Jesus?" A New Testament critic from the University of Notre Dame was quoted: "Jesus expected a radical transformation of the world and that this would involve the coming of a heavenly figure . . . but Jesus did not believe himself to be this figure."[6]

If Jesus didn't believe in Himself, how can we? No wonder mankind today is groaning under pressure. The hope of the ages is being scorned by the humanists who stubbornly believe we can create a New Age of love and harmony by our own efforts.

I've never seen a crazier time. What seems to be, isn't. What doesn't seem to be, is. But this I know: He's in charge.

The Overcomers

We are living in a time when we like to hear only the positive. Although I am a positive thinker, I know that there will be wars and rumors of wars until Jesus Christ ends them forever. We don't like war, we don't advocate war, but it is an inevitable fact of existence.

In 1849 Ralph Waldo Emerson wrote: "War is on its last legs; and a universal peace is as sure as is the prevalence of civilization over barbarism."[7] Since that time there have been two world wars and more local wars, civil insurrections, and revolutions than we could count.

Emerson was wrong, just as many others have been. John's Revelation is a militant book. It reverberates with the sound of armies and the noise of battle. We are told "There was war in heaven" (12:7). Except for God's special chosen ones, no one will survive. The might of all hell will battle against Christ and His overcomers—the martyrs whom the devil tries to destroy.

"Overcome" is a strong word. It means to conquer or win a victory. It's used in the Bible for winning lawsuits, wars, moral battles, and spiritual conflicts. The greatest people I have ever known have been those who overcame personal difficulties in what looked like impossible situations. God has promised that we can all be overcomers, even the weakest of us, and overcomers receive rich rewards.

"He who has an ear, let him hear what the Spirit says to the churches. *To him who overcomes, I will give the right to eat from the tree of life, which is in the paradise of God"* (Revelation 2:7, emphasis added).

"To him who overcomes, I will give the right to sit with me on my throne, just as I overcame and sat down with my Father on his throne" (Revelation 3:21, emphasis added).

"He who overcomes shall inherit all this, and I will be his God and he will be my son" (Revelation 21:7, emphasis added).

Peace and safety will come, but not through man's efforts. The blessings will be for the overcomers, the victors in the last war on earth.

An old man on a remote island was given the inspiration and information to write the greatest cover story of all time. The preface to that story is being written in the closing days of the Second Millennium.

3

VISION OF
AN EXILE

A loud knock on the door—the sound of angry voices—frightened people inside, knowing the encounter they had dreaded was happening. They are placed under arrest, their destiny unknown.

Aleksandr Solzhenitsyn, who knew both the terror of imprisonment and the humiliation of exile, wrote: "Arrest! Need it be said that it is a breaking point in your life, a bolt of lightning which has scored a direct hit on you? It is an unassimilable spiritual earthquake not every person can cope with, as a result of which people often slip into insanity."[1]

After John's arrest by Roman soldiers, did he lose his sanity? Were his body and his mind so battered by the stark cruelty of banishment to that barren isle of Patmos that he became paranoid? After all, he was an old man, deprived of family and friends, thrown among thieves and murderers to scratch out an existence on an island stained with the blood of victims. Before exile most prisoners were beaten and tortured, denied warm clothing or adequate food, so John may have been in poor physical condition.

He had been the leader of Roman believers and a clear witness for Jesus. It was logical that the Emperor Domitian would want to destroy him and weaken his testimony. To kill him would have meant the silencing of just another Christian martyr, but to force him to beg for mercy and deny this Christ he followed would have been a victory. John himself had written in his Gospel that in the world believers would have tribulation. Even though he was the "disciple whom Jesus loved," he was not immune to suffering.[2]

Out of the suffering of God's people have come some of the greatest triumphs. When circumstances look darkest, God has the opportunity to shine the brightest.

John was not insane; he was the one person God entrusted to reveal the end of this present age and the beginning of a new world.

Ups and Downs in the Life of John

John told the churches that he was a "brother and companion in the suffering and kingdom and patient endurance that are ours in Jesus" (Revelation 1:9).

So many of us cry, "Why me?" when problems pile one upon another. The question should probably be, "Why not me?" Why should we be exempt from trials? John had every right to bemoan his fate; he had been a faithful follower of the Master, but in spite of his loyalty, he was a common prisoner. He could have buried his head and moaned, "What did I do to deserve this?"

But John was "in the Spirit," yielding himself to the Lord's direction. It was then that he saw Him—a vision of such awesome majesty that he passed out! I probably would have, too.

No Artist Could Paint Him

From the time I was a little boy, looking at the pictures of Jesus surrounded by children, carrying a lamb on His shoulder, or hanging limply on a cross, I have loved Him. I knew the image I had in my mind: He had long, light brown hair, blue eyes, a thin face, and a slender body. He was my Midwest Sunday school image of Jesus.

Time magazine printed on its cover a composite of artists' impressions of Jesus, from surrealistic angular drawings to bland, expressionless tapestries. Jesus has been the subject of more painters than any other person in history.

John did not see the lowly Galilean of the Gospels, but he saw a picture of the glorified Christ who will establish His kingdom on earth in the future. We can imagine Jesus as the rugged man who walked the hills of Judea and spoke without a microphone to thousands in Galilee, but our minds are incapable of grasping John's vision.

John writes that "On the Lord's Day I was in the Spirit" (Revelation 1:10) and most of us think it must have been Sunday. How could that old man have recorded this book in one day? "The Lord's Day" is a reference to the Day of the Lord, a term found often in the Old Testament, and describes an extended period of time in which God is the sovereign ruler over the earth.[3]

The normal limitations of John's mind and body were laid aside and he was projected into the future. We can take the same journey.

Portrait of the Future

John goes on: "I turned around to see the voice that was speaking to me. And when I turned I saw seven golden lampstands, and among the lampstands was someone 'like a son of man,' dressed in a robe reaching down to his feet and with a golden sash around his chest. His head and hair were white like wool, as white as snow, and his eyes were like blazing fire. His feet were like bronze glowing in a furnace, and his voice was like the sound of rushing waters. In his right hand he held seven stars, and out of his mouth came a sharp double-edged sword.

His face was like the sun shining in all its brilliance" (Revelation 1:12–16).

John was electrified; he collapsed, frozen in time and space. He saw the universe from a heavenly viewpoint, and experienced the presence of Jesus as we shall see Him some day.

Jesus stood among "seven golden lampstands," which He explained later were the seven churches. Lampstands, of course, light our way at night. When Christ was banished from the world, the world was plunged into darkness; however, the lampstands, representing the churches, throw their light on His perfections. The light is the Lord's, not the churches, and the purpose of the light is to bring glory to the Father in heaven.

"Let your light so shine before men, that they may see your good deeds and praise your Father in heaven" (Matthew 5:16), said Jesus. The responsibility of Christians is to let a lost world see the light of the glory of God. Church programs are fine, if Christ is at the center. Sunday school lessons may relate to immediate personal problems, if Jesus is the focus. The ultimate success or failure of social concerns, charity groups, or philanthropic organizations depends upon that focus.

In my ministry, as it is with any Christian organization, we become involved with fund-raising events, media outreach, and charitable drives. Details multiply like a flu virus and the fever soars. Just when we think we are the hub in the center of the wheel, we are reminded that Jesus walks in the midst of the churches. When I look out on my congregation, I shudder to think that Jesus might be sitting in the back row, when His position must be in the place of prominence, the center, where everyone can see Him.

Every stroke of the Spirit's brush has a meaning. John saw Him in a long flowing robe that speaks of His greatness. The prophet Isaiah wrote, ". . . I saw the Lord seated on a throne high and exalted, and the train of his robe filled the temple" (Isaiah 6:1).

As a minister I've conducted many weddings where the bride had a long train, sweeping the white runner on the church aisle. To see a robe that filled an entire temple would be impressive.

The golden sash across His chest is a symbol of His righteousness. We read of Jesus girding Himself with a towel and washing the disciples' feet, but here He is clothed in majesty, not as a servant. Isaiah said, "Righteousness will be his belt and faithfulness the sash around his waist" (Isaiah 11:5).

His eyes were like blazing fire, contrasting with His time on earth when John had seen Him with tear-filled eyes. He looks into the deepest depths of the soul, penetrating every thought and motive. The Bible says, "Nothing in all creation is hidden from God's sight. Everything is uncovered and laid bare before the eyes of him to whom we must give account" (Hebrews 4:13). When someone who is living a holy, Christ-filled life looks into my eyes, I know I cannot hide behind any facade.

"His feet were like bronze glowing in a furnace . . ." (Revelation 1:15). Brass (or bronze) represents judgment. The feet of brass signify the time when He will put all His enemies and every evil power beneath his feet. The foes of Jesus will be utterly crushed. If I didn't know that, I would have to join all the moaners who wail, "I just don't know what this world is coming to!"

"His voice was like the sound of rushing waters" (Revelation 1:15). This is not a quiet stream, but a booming Niagara Falls. Jeremiah was given this prophecy: "The Lord will roar on high; he will thunder from his holy dwelling and roar mightily against his land. . . . The tumult will resound to the ends of the earth" (Jeremiah 25:30, 31). An old expression puts it this way: "It was so loud my teeth rattled." The sound of His voice will shake the corners of heaven and earth.

Out of His mouth "came a sharp double-edged sword," an instrument of warfare that is the Word of God. "For the word of God is living and active. Sharper than any double-edged sword, it penetrates even to dividing soul and spirit, joints and marrow; it judges the thoughts and attitudes of the heart" (Hebrews 4:12).

When Billy Graham raises his Bible and emphasizes, "The Bible says . . ." he is using the sword of the Spirit. Every time we look to the Scriptures for answers and direction, we are warring against evil. Satan hates to have us quote Scripture. He loves it when men question the truth of the Bible—or twist the meaning to match their own beliefs.

In the book of Revelation, the two-edged sword is the weapon of our Lord. We see a mighty warrior, battling the forces of evil to a final victory. We may not be able to paint a picture of such awesome proportions, but we can know the Conqueror is on our side and that gives us great assurance.

"In his right hand he held seven stars" (Revelation 1:16). In the Bible the right hand represents authority and control. Jesus is described in the Scriptures as sitting on the right hand of God. The seven stars are identified in following verses as seven angels. The stars of the churches are His ambassadors, the pastors or ministers over whom the Lord exercises absolute authority, and those whom He protects when they obey Him and are faithful in His service.

If John had looked directly into the face of the Lord, he might have been blinded, for "His face was like the sun shining in all its brilliance" (Revelation 1:16). The face of the Lord is the central feature of His person—it represents everything that He is. Everything fades in light of its brilliance.

I can imagine John in his tattered prison garb, viewing the majesty of the man he knew in Judea and losing consciousness. This was an instinctive human reaction of fear. Others in the Bible experienced the same fear: Abraham fell on his face when God talked with him; Moses hid his face for he was afraid; Balaam bowed his head and fell flat on his face; Isaiah saw the Lord seated on a throne in the temple and cried, "Woe to me: . . . I am ruined!" The three disciples who saw His face shine as the sun fell on their faces, too. Remember Saul of Tarsus? He dropped to the ground and was blinded.[4]

It shouldn't surprise us that John fainted. He was overwhelmed by the majesty of the glorified Son of Man.

The Touch That Takes Away Fear

Have you ever been so afraid that you seemed paralyzed? Fear is a normal emotion, and doctors tell us that people can die as a result of a frightening encounter. Heart attacks are not uncommon in situations where people are terrified. But the Lord touched John and spoke to him with such assurance that John must have awakened and been calmed by His soothing words. How can Jesus take away our fear?

He said to John and He says to us: "I am the First and the Last. I am the Living One" (Revelation 1:17).

No one was before Jesus. He has existed since eternity past and will *be* for all eternity future. If our sole emphasis is upon the historical Jesus, great communicator and teacher, this concept is impossible to grasp.

Jesus said, "I am the Living One." If we know that fact, the touch of His hand can take away our fears.

A story is told about an elderly woman who was saved by her two dogs from freezing to death. She had gone outside on a brutally cold Oklahoma night and slipped on the bare concrete of her patio. As she ran a shaking hand across her hip, she realized that it was broken. She was unable to move, and no one was in calling distance. She cried to God to help her, knowing that she couldn't survive the night in those bitter temperatures. Suddenly she remembered the words that Paul had written in prison when he was waiting to die: "That is why I am suffering as I am. Yet I am not ashamed, because I know whom I have believed, and am convinced that he is able to guard what I have entrusted to him for that day" (2 Timothy 1:12).

She prayed, "Father God, I'm suffering out here in this cold, and I don't believe You'll let me freeze to death. I am trusting You to save me, but whether I live or die, I believe in Jesus."

Jesus touched her, not with human hands, but through her two Labrador retrievers, who pulled a blanket over her, and then pressed their warm bodies against her throughout the cold night. She survived, and she says that when she prayed her fear left her and she felt the assuring presence of Jesus.[5]

Jesus tells us not to fear because He is the resurrected Christ; He is alive for ever and ever. I often think that we should give the same intensity of celebration to Easter as we do to Christmas. Without the resurrection of Christ, our faith would be hollow and we would have much to fear.

As the leaders of world religions die, what do their followers do? Since they can no longer find strength in a man, they must look for some other source of hope. Ours is a living hope.

Jesus told John not to be afraid because He holds the keys of death and Hades. Our future is in His hands and He has victory over death and the grave.

Billy Graham wrote: "Whatever suffering and agony we must endure, either in our own body or for someone we love, we are assured of His presence. And ultimately we will be resurrected with a body free of pain, an incorruptible and immortal body like His. This is our future hope."[6]

Many people have claimed to have visions. Some get that glazed, other-worldly look in their eyes and intone with hushed voices about the insight they have into the meaning of present events or future happenings. John, the prisoner of Patmos, was not suffering from hallucinations. He saw and recorded events that will shape the future of every one of the earth's billions.

Revelation can knock us out of our complacency, out of our fear of the future and into confident living.

Part II

THE WORLD TODAY:
Ruined by Man

4

THE CHURCH
UNDER GLASS

Some people don't think churches are important. "I have my private way of worshiping—I don't need four walls and a preacher," they say.

God thinks churches are important and when He gave John the vision, it was almost as if He were looking through a magnifying glass at our churches today.

The world is full of churches; in almost every one of our American towns there's a white church with a steeple, a stone church covered with vines, a modern church built at angles, and usually the church with the most impressive stained-glass windows.

Some churches have chairs down the aisles and people standing in the foyer; in others the pastor stares over empty rows to reach the eyes of the timid souls in the back.

God is not a member of one denomination or another. When Jesus was teaching His disciples He asked them, "'Who do you say I am?' Peter answered, 'You are the Christ, the Son of the living God.' Jesus replied, 'Blessed are you, Simon son of

Jonah, for this was not revealed to you by man, but by my Father in heaven. And I tell you that you are Peter, and on this rock I will build my church, and the gates of Hades will not overcome it'" (Matthew 16:15–18).

The Rock upon which the church is built is not Peter. The Rock is Christ Himself, as Paul clearly said, ". . . and that rock was Christ" (1 Corinthians 10:4).

The only true church is made up of individuals who have accepted Jesus Christ as Savior. Within every church building or denominational structure there are true members of the church and there are others who call themselves church members simply because they are in the directory.

Jesus wrote seven letters to seven literal churches in Asia Minor during the first century. However, these letters have not been assigned to the national archives to gather dust. They are as current as today's calendar, and they offer a chronological account of church history.

These churches were real; people attended services in them and listened to the messages. Although the letters were written in the first century, they apply to our contemporary churches and have personal value to every believer. The letters begin with the first century church and end with the last type of church which will be on earth at the end of the age.

Church Shopping

How do we choose a church home? Many churches believe they must have a dynamic, young, good-looking pastor with a wife who raises three beautiful children, plays the piano, and conducts a weekly Bible class. Other churches think they will attract the masses with a lavish sanctuary, a magnificent pipe organ, or a well-equipped kitchen. However, none of these influence a church's growth or decline as significantly as how much love and acceptance people experience when they attend.

The Institute for American Church Growth in Pasadena (California) conducted a survey of 8,600 people from congregations in thirty-nine denominations to measure their "love-care" quotient. Here's what they learned: members of growing churches are more loving to each other and to visitors. Loving churches, regardless of their theology, denomination, or location—attract more people.

The first church of Ephesus had some serious love problems, just as some modern churches do.

Letter to Ephesus: The Evangelical Church

Ephesus was one of the urban centers in the Roman empire. It was a cosmopolitan city of rich and poor, cultured and ignorant, a gathering place for false religious cults and superstitions. The temple of Diana, one of the seven wonders of the world, was there. This shrine served as the bank of Asia, an art gallery, and a sanctuary for criminals; the city derived much of its wealth from the manufacture and sale of images of the goddess.

The letter began on a positive note:

"I know your deeds, your hard work and your perseverance. I know that you cannot tolerate wicked men, that you have tested those who claim to be apostles but are not, and found them false. You have persevered and have endured hardships for my name, and have not grown weary" (Revelation 2:2, 3).

When Paul made Ephesus a center for evangelism during the three years he spent there, the church apparently flourished. After Paul's release from prison, he probably visited the city again and established Timothy as the pastor. John may have succeeded Timothy. A fairly impressive group of ministers, wouldn't you say?

The Ephesian congregation was dynamic and its annual report must have looked good. It would never have matched this report I saw recently: "Annual report . . . New members: none. Baptisms: none. Gifts to missions: none." Then at the bottom of the report the church clerk had written, "Brethren, pray for us that we might be faithful unto the end."

The Ephesian church persevered through times of trouble. One of my heroes in the faith is Charles Spurgeon. He said: "Pray God to send a few men with what the Americans call 'grit' in them; men, who when they know a thing to be right, will not turn away, or turn aside, or stop; men who will persevere all the more because there are difficulties to meet or foes to encounter."[1]

Church discipline was prevalent in the Ephesian church. If someone falsely claimed to be an apostle, he was called a liar. Today there are churches where the leaders claim to be apostles. The Ephesians would not have accepted those men; they were careful to examine visiting ministers to see if they were genuine.

They also despised the Nicolaitans, a sect which led a life of self-indulgence and immorality. A true love for God involves a fervent aversion to those who counterfeit and distort the purity of biblical truth.

Sounds like a great church, doesn't it? It was dynamic, dedicated, patient, disciplined, and discerning. But Jesus saw past all the pious facade; the church of Ephesus had heart trouble!

"Yet I hold this against you: You have forsaken your first love" (Revelation 3:4).

What a shock to be told that you don't love Christ as you once did. Love should grow, not wither. One commentator wrote: "To have something against friend or brother may be very human . . . But when it is the Lord who has something against the church, it is time to tremble; and when that thing is loss of love, the church should not only tremble, it should fall on its knees."[2]

These Ephesians (and the spiritual Ephesians of our time) had stopped loving Christ and each other the way they once had done.

We hear the same about marriage. "I just don't love him any more," the wife complains to a counselor. What happened to the girl whose heart beat faster when she heard his car outside? Where is the man who used to bring flowers and tell her how lucky he was to have found her? The "Ephesian" marriages have lost the thrill of first love.

Once the diagnosis has been made, the prescription can be written. Here are three steps to renewing love:

First, *remember* what it was like. Relive the thrill of romance, the desire to tell the world of its wonder. When I see the tears of joy in the eyes of men, women, and children who have accepted Jesus as Savior, when I perform a marriage and see the transformation on the faces of that couple as they look at each other, I want to touch them and say, "Beloved, don't lose your first love."

Second, *repent* and turn your life around. Make a conscious vow to make that relationship right again.

Third, *repeat*—"do the things you did at first"—those acts of love, even if you don't feel like it. Do it and the feelings will follow.

Talk about revival in the church, or in a marriage! It can explode!

Jesus warned the church at Ephesus that it would lose its light and its testimony in the community, if the first love was not revived (Revelation 2:5). This actually happened many years later when Ephesus declined as a city. It is now uninhabited and one of the major ruins of the area.

What a warning this is to churches that have lost their first love. When my wife and I were in Europe we visited beautiful churches with graveyard interiors. We went to the great tabernacle in London where Charles Spurgeon once preached to overflow audiences. My heart was saddened to sit in that vast worship hall with less than a hundred people in attendance.

Surrounding us in every country are church buildings which are no more than clerical caskets, lined in rich satin, gilded with gold, and buried in complacency.

Looking at the outside, the church at Ephesus appeared to be a model church. However, inside the love was growing cold, the people were involved in their "good works" out of a sense of duty. The historical era of this church was A.D. 33–100.

Christ ends every one of His letters to the churches with the same conclusion: "He who has an ear, let him hear what the Spirit says to the churches" (Revelation 2:7).

Are we able to hear the warning signs that we are losing our first love? Where is the excitement we experienced as new believers in Jesus Christ? Where is the thrill of looking at the wife or husband we adored when we were first married? *Love is abused when it is not used.*

In our busy lives we may allow our love relationship with the Lord to grow weak. The church at Ephesus has an important message for us: the Lord is to have priority in our lives. Personally, I could stop at the first letter and have my heart burn with conviction. I know there are times when I slip into Ephesus, and I do not like the atmosphere.

Letter to Smyrna: The Iron Curtain Church

Corrie ten Boom recalled a childhood incident when she told her father, "I am afraid that I will never be strong enough to die as a martyr."

He said, "When you have to go on a journey, when do I give you the money for the fare—two weeks before?"

"No, Daddy, on the day that I am leaving."

"Precisely . . . and our wise Father in heaven knows when we're going to need things, too. When the time comes to die, you will find the strength you need—just in time."

In later years, Corrie was imprisoned in Ravensbruk, the infamous German prison camp where more than 50,000 women were killed. She wrote, "It is necessary, when we prepare ourselves for the end-time, also to be prepared to die for Jesus."[3]

Living in a country where we are not tortured or killed for our faith in Jesus, it seems remote that we might be called upon to be martyrs. However, martyrdom is not just a tortur-ing death. What if we lose our jobs because we're Christians? What if our children are taunted because they believe in Jesus Christ? Suffering takes many forms.

The letter to the church at Smyrna was personally written to people under pressure. Every word He speaks to this suffer-ing body is one of appreciation. Only two of the seven churches received letters of total commendation and encouragement: Smyrna is one and Philadelphia is the other.

Smyrna was the proudest and most beautiful city of Asia. It is considered by historians as the most exquisite city the Greeks ever built. The city sloped to the sea, and along the sides of the hill was a large amphitheater, where over 20,000 people could sit. It was there that the worship of Caesar was centered.

By the time the book of Revelation was written, emperor worship was compulsory. The churches were persecuted be-cause they wouldn't bow down to Caesar and burn incense in the temple dedicated to *Kaiser Kurios,* Caesar is Lord!

The Christians who refused to obey the emperor's decree were marked men, traitors against the government. To be a Christian in the Roman Empire during that bloody era was to live in jeopardy every day; the tortures inflicted on these men of faith were despicable. Some Christians were strapped on the rack (a wheel about two feet wide and eight feet tall), their ankles chained to the floor and wrists tied to the wheel. Every time the believer was asked to deny the Lord and refused, the rack was tightened until he was ripped limb for limb. Other Christians were thrown into boiling oil, or mangled by hungry lions in the coliseum.

The church at Smyrna was pulled apart by pressure, poverty, and persecution. Most of us cannot comprehend what it would be like to have our fingernails torn out or to see our children slaughtered before our eyes. Jesus gave two com-mands to this suffering family. He told them to be fearless, just as David wrote in those famous words, "Even though I walk through the valley of the shadow of death, I will fear no evil" (Psalm 23).

He told the believers in Smyrna to be faithful, even to the point of death. Are we, at the human level, capable of such sacrifice?

The Church in Today's Catacombs is a book that documents the stories of people who suffered under the brutality of the communist regime, or had been eyewitnesses to the suffering of others. The brutal acts performed on these martyrs were so inhuman we could not repeat the obscenities our Christian brothers and sisters endured behind the Iron Curtain.

Suzanne Labin wrote: ". . . Romans, Mongolians, and Hitlerites did not torture their own followers. Communism has set this last precedent. It has killed with the worst sufferings ten thousand times as many Communists as have all the anti-Communist regimes put together. Even wolves do not devour each other. But Communists do. It is a madman's world."[4]

The Christians at Smyrna lived in a world where they were despised for their faith. Christ encouraged them by telling them that through every trial they would ever have, He understood. The one who was slandered, falsely accused, whipped, brutally beaten, and hung upon a Roman cross said, "I know your afflictions and your poverty—yet you are rich!" (Revelation 2:9).

He knew persecution and poverty, and yet He reminded His followers that they were rich! The Lord's values are different from those of the world.

He said, "you will suffer persecution for ten days" (Revelation 2:10). I believe the intent of His words was to prepare the church for the suffering that would be brief in contrast to eternity.

The pastor of the church in Smyrna was a student and disciple of John. His name was Polycarp, and he was the messenger (angel) of whom Christ spoke when John wrote this second letter. Polycarp's ministry ended in A.D. 156 when persecution of Christians increased and they were tortured and thrown to the wild beasts. Polycarp was marched into the amphitheater where a mob was waiting to see what form of ghoulish pleasure they could get from his violent death. As he stood before the proconsul, he was commanded to deny Christ, but he replied, "Eighty-six years have I served Him and He never did me any harm; how then can I blaspheme my King and my Savior?"

As the old man stood before the crowd in the stadium, the governor shouted, "I'll have you destroyed by fire, unless you change your attitude."

Polycarp answered: "You threaten me with fire which burns for an hour and after a little is extinguished. But you are ignorant of the fires of the coming judgment and of eternal punishment reserved for the ungodly. But why do you delay? Bring on what you will."

The crowd gathered wood and threw torches on the pyre. Their hatred was bitter and they cheered as the godly man was brought to the stake. As the flames began to curl around his body, Polycarp prayed:

"I thank you that you have graciously thought me worthy of this day and of this hour, that I may be a part of the number of martyrs to die for Christ."[5]

Perhaps we have become so refined in our teaching of Bible truths that we are softening the shouts of the martyrs. Christians throughout time have been persecuted for their faith. Some of us today may be called upon to suffer in our own lifetimes.

Letter to Pergamum: The Inner City Church

Times Square in New York City spills the putrid breath of its porno shops, X-rated movies, prostitutes, and drug dealers into neon-lit streets. Enticements can beckon in subtle ways with promises of easy love and cheap thrills. Every town, school, and business houses the potential of Satan's city.

If we had entered Pergamum, the capitol of Asia, we

might have been caught breathless by its beauty. It was built on a rocky hill, where the Mediterranean could be seen on a clear day (it probably wasn't plagued by smog). Pergamum was a cultural center, famous for its library that was said to house 200,000 rolls of parchment. I imagine the city attracted the finest minds in the academic world. However, Jesus didn't write to the professors in their ivory towers, but to Christians, struggling to keep their faith amidst the critics of higher learning. He called Pergamum "Satan's city," which may not have pleased the professors and bibliophiles.

The city was deeply entrenched in the worship of the god of healing, and the temples of Asclepius were like the hospitals in the ancient world. The emblem of Asclepius was the coiled snake that appeared on many of the coins of the city. Today, the coiled snake on a staff is the insignia of the medical profession. Perhaps our doctors might not want to know that the symbol originated in Satan's city!

The believers in that city may have been like Christians today who sit in classrooms and listen to learned teachers scoff at Christian beliefs or undercut their values. They were commended because ". . . you remain true to my name. You did not renounce your faith in me, even in the days of Antipas, my faithful witness . . ." (Revelation 2:12). (Antipas was slowly roasted to death in a bronze kettle.)

However, Christ said, "Nevertheless, I have a few things against you" (Revelation 2:14). The Pergamum believers may have looked at each other and said, "What have we done?" They had become compromisers. Satan did not make a frontal attack by coming in as a roaring lion (1 Peter 5:8). He slithered in the back door and led them astray as a deceiving serpent.

Jesus told them there were certain members of the Pergamum congregation who were following weird teaching. Some were listening to doctrines of Balaam, and others to the Nicolaitans (Revelation 2:14, 15).

In each of the churches so far, Satan has had a different strategy. The Ephesian church had lost its first love. In Smyrna, the cruelty of Satan came from outside forces. In Pergamum, Satan used the approach Balaam used against Israel.

Balaam was a prophet who said he could influence the gods for or against men by his incantations and offerings. He ran a wholesale business in divine favors, so Balak, king of Moab, offered Balaam a nice profit if he could bring down a curse on the king's despised enemies in Israel.

Balaam tried to command God, but instead of a curse, Israel was blessed. Balaam's plan backfired. Frustrated by his failure to get what he wanted, he showed Balak how he could corrupt Israel by having the adulterous Moabite women seduce the Israelite men. This plan worked, and Balaam was the prime mover in the fall of Israel. His tactic was, "If you can't curse them, corrupt them" (Numbers 22–25).

The sin of Pergamum, just as that of Balaam, was the toleration of evil. Worldly standards had crept into their fellowship. Today it's the same worldly spirit within the church which makes it difficult to distinguish between the actions of Christians and the lifestyles of non-Christians. When those who call themselves Christians commit adultery, cheat in business, or lower their moral standards to suit the situation, they fit into the Pergamum mentality.

The compromising Christians in Pergamum heard the same command that is heard today: "Repent therefore!"

God gives His rewards for turning our lives from compromise to commitment. He loves us enough to forgive us, but He will not force that love upon us.

After the call for repentance, there are two promises from the Lord: "I will give some of the hidden manna. I will also give him a white stone with a new name written on it, known only to him who receives it" (Revelation 2:17).

"Hidden manna" from heaven is the nourishment needed for spiritual health. I remember as a seminary student in Dallas, I worked in a freight yard. The job was hard physical labor and my working companions used pretty raw language and jokes. One day, during our lunch break, I noticed a new fellow hunched in a corner with his "hidden manna," a well-worn New Testament. He chose not to compromise, no matter what surrounded him.

In ancient courts, white and black stones signified the verdicts of juries. A black stone meant guilty; a white stone meant acquittal. The Christian is acquitted in the sight of God because of the work of Jesus Christ. The verdict is not guilty.

Modern counterparts to members of the church in Pergamum have muddied their Christian commitment with compromise. So much of the world is in the church and so many of the church are in the world that there is no difference between the two.

The Pergamum period of history evolved into an era when Christianity was introduced by force.

The "Christian Emperor"

Ephesus represents the period of the apostles; Smyrna represents the period of persecution during the second and third centuries. When Diocletian, the last persecuting emperor of that era, failed to stamp out the church, Constantine came into power. Tradition has it that Constantine looked up and saw a vision in the shape of a cross which said, *in hoc signo vinces:* "By this sign conquer." That night, Constantine bargained with Satan to join the church and declare himself a Christian. Christianity, said Emperor Constantine, was to be the religion of the state.

Christian leaders were invited to watch the wholesale baptism of entire regiments of soldiers in Constantine's army. Christianity was forced on unwilling subjects at sword point: baptism or death! The unholy alliance of church and state resulted.

In the early part of the third century, the Pergamum church was married to the world. True believers, who had been previously persecuted, were now lauded by political and civil authorities. Constantine assumed leadership of the church; pagan temples became Christian churches; heathen festivals were converted into Christian ones. Idols were named after so-called Christian saints. Many Christians who had suffered were now welcomed to the imperial palace and they swallowed the bait, sacrificing allegiance to Christ, and becoming locked in fatal union with compromise. Constantine was now called Pontifex Maximus and assumed leadership of the church.

Out of this alliance between the Roman emperor and the Christian church came the birth of Roman Catholicism.

Letter to Thyatira: The Suburban Church

The next church to receive an important letter was in Thyatira, a place quite the opposite of Ephesus. Instead of shriveled love, it had growing love; the people worked hard, faithfully, and patiently. Beneath the healthy surface, however, was a cesspool.

A modern man, cut in the mold of the Thyatiran church, received a memo on his desk, requesting his appearance at two o'clock in the boss's office. At 1:59 he walked in, wiping his sweaty palms on his sides. After a pleasant greeting, the boss said, "Sit down, I want to tell you some positive things I've observed about your work." The fellow eased himself into the chair in front of the executive desk and the knot in his stomach began to dissolve. Maybe he'd get a raise.

"You're a good worker, and you seem to believe strongly in what you're doing."

A grin crossed his face as he tried to be humble about his achievements. All the overtime hadn't been in vain.

"Nevertheless," the boss continued, "I have evidence that you are frequently seen with a woman who is not your wife."

The man behind the desk seemed to have eyes that could look right through the accused employee. Adultery may not be an indictment in many companies, but in this case the worker was the youth pastor in a large church.

When Jesus wrote the letter to the pastor of the church in Thyatira He said, "I know your deeds, your love and faith, your service and perseverance, and that you are now doing more than you did at first. Nevertheless I have this against you . . ." (Revelation 2:19). Now the tone changes. Outward conduct may be exemplary, but we can't fool Him. His burning eyes pierce the darkness and flash with the flame of moral anger.

Joseph Seiss wrote: "There is nothing more piercing than flaming fire. Everything yields and melts before it. It penetrates all things, consumes every opposition, sweeps down all obstructions, and presses its way with invincible power. And of this sort are the eyes of Jesus. They look through everything; they pierce through all masks and coverings; they search the remotest recesses; they behold the most hidden things of the soul; and there is no escape from them."[6]

In many ways, the service of Thyatira was better than that of the previous churches. Thyatira had the love that Ephesus had abandoned; the believers there preserved the faith that was in jeopardy in Pergamos and shared with Smyrna the patience needed to endure suffering. Instead of backsliding, the church was going forward. However, in the beautiful body of this church, a cancer was allowed to grow.

John Stott has reminded us of Satan's strategy: "If the devil cannot conquer the church by the application of political pressure or the propagation of intellectual heresy, he will try the insinuation of moral evil. This was the dragon's strategy in Thyatira."[7]

Lounging seductively behind the facade of piety was "that woman Jezebel." The real Jezebel had been dead for nearly a thousand years, but her prototype was a prophetess who had become prominent in Thyatira.

Historically, Jezebel was the wife of Ahab, one of Israel's most wicked kings. When she married Ahab, she brought her brand of religion with her and persuaded her husband to build a temple to Astarte, the goddess whose religion made sexual immorality a part of "worship."

Jezebel (and what little girl is ever given that infamous name today?) supported over 800 prophets of her immoral cult and killed all the prophets of Jehovah that she could find. Weak-kneed old Ahab didn't have the spiritual courage to stop his wicked wife. Jezebel's character was so evil that Elijah the prophet prophesied she would come to a sudden end and her body would be eaten by dogs. Jezebel was the epitome of immorality and idolatry.

Thyatira tolerated a satanic woman in its midst and refused to censor her. The Christians in Thyatira had either a poor conscience or very weak courage; their refusal to rebuke their Jezebel was like Ahab's refusal to deal with his.

Christ, always patient and desiring people to turn from their wicked ways, gave this adulterous woman time to repent, but she refused. He issued a dire warning; His message to the cult was severe. He said He would "cast her on a bed of suffering, and I will make those who commit adultery with her suffer intensely, unless they repent of her ways" (Revelation 2:22).

Literal punishments of sickness and death were to be inflicted upon the spiritual children of this cultic family. This truth about our Lord ought to be a sobering reminder that He looks past the facade and sees us for what we are.

Not everyone in the church of Thyatira had become a part of this evil cult; to this group of Christians, Christ gives some marvelous promises. He tells them to hold on to their faith until He returns.

It's encouraging to know that a remnant of this type of church will rule someday with Christ in His earthly kingdom. Hope is always present in the midst of the worst circumstances!

Sardis: The Liberal Church

A certain minister had a reputation for being eccentric. One Sunday morning, he told his congregation that he believed his church was dead. You can imagine the murmurings from the pews when he said, "Come back tonight, I'm going to preach the funeral service of the church." The members were shocked; the attendance for the evening service was larger than it had been in years.

In front of the pews was a casket and as the people sat in stunned silence, the pastor delivered the message. After the last "amen," the pastor said, "Some of you may not agree with me that this church is dead. So that you may be convinced, I am going to ask you to view the remains. I want you to file by the casket, one by one, and see who is dead."

In preparation for this unorthodox presentation, the minister had placed a mirror in the bottom of the casket. It is obvious who everyone saw when he came to view the deceased.

I would not recommend this technique, but the point is effective.

No Praise for Cold Sardians

This letter had a different tone from previous letters. For the poor, but rich, church in Smyrna, our Lord had nothing but words of praise. For the churches of Ephesus, Pergamos, and Thyatira, He had a mixture of praise and criticism. To the majority of the church at Sardis, He said nothing praiseworthy. Sardis may have been the first church in history to have been filled with what we call "nominal Christians." Sardis appeared to be alive, but was dead. The Lord is never impressed by the beauty of a well-kept mausoleum, knowing that inside are the bones of a dead man.

When John wrote this letter to Sardis, it was a wealthy city, but degenerate. Twice the city had been lost because the leadership and the citizenry were too lazy to defend themselves from their enemies. The attitude of the city was reflected in the demise of its church. Like the city that smugly dwelt upon its past glory, the church at Sardis had won a good reputation at one time and the members thought they had arrived; they were content in the beautiful building they had erected on the corner of Self-satisfaction and Complacency steets.

"I know your deeds; you have a reputation of being alive, but you are dead" (Revelation 3:1), Jesus wrote.

A spiritual autopsy of Sardis will show us the causes of death. First, Sardis died because it relied on its past successes. The body which was once healthy had been neglected. Second, the church died because it allowed sin to creep into the membership. Herodotus, the historian, records that over the course of many years the church in Sardis had acquired a reputation for lax moral standards. Third, the church died because it was not sensitive to its own spiritual condition; it was confident that God was there because the building was magnificent and the parishioners were well-dressed. They were like the people Paul described in his letter to young Timothy: ". . . having a form of godliness but denying its power" (2 Timothy 3:5).

John Stott reminds us that hypocrisy like this can permeate the whole life of a church:

"We can have a fine choir, an expensive organ, good music, great anthems, and fine congregational singing. We can mouth hymns and psalms with unimpeachable elegance, while our mind wanders and our heart is far from God. We can have pomp and ceremony, color and ritual, liturgical exactness and ecclesiastic splendor, and yet be offering a worship which is not perfect or 'fulfilled' in the sight of God."[8]

What Can We Do If Our Church Is Dead?

The letter to Sardis says, "Wake up!" Shake out of your smug, brick-walled, stained-glass complacency. Christ is not just saying to the church to wake from its death sleep, He is calling upon it to remain awake.

The first call toward renewal is the honest awareness that something is wrong. Churches die spiritually because Christians allow doctrinal error to slip into the membership. I've often had someone say, "Why do we have membership classes or examination of our beliefs before we're allowed to join a church? Anyone who wants to join should be allowed to do so." What if a teacher who believes in evolution becomes a member without any profession of faith? The Sunday school superintendent, eager to have a teacher for the fourth through six grades, asks the new member to take the classes. What are those children going to be taught?

Doctrine not important? It's vital.

Christ's warning to the church is sobering: "But if you do not wake up, I will come like a thief, and you will not know at what time I will come to you" (Revelation 3:3). I believe this is warning against the sudden judgment which God would bring upon this individual church if it did not watch and repent.

However, in the church at Sardis, and in our own Sardian-type churches today, there are a few who have remained true to Christ. There is never a day so dark that God does not have His stars—His men. In the days before the flood, God had righteous Enoch and Noah. In the time of universal idolatry, there was Abraham. Even in Sodom, there was Lot.

What should we do if we are members of a dead or dying church? Christ reminds the true believer of the importance of the Holy Spirit, to be submissive to His control. Some will be led out of that church, others will remain and hold fast.

Should I Stay or Should I Leave?

In the ancient city of Sardis there may not have been another Christian church, dead or alive. Today, believers have choices. For those within the church at Sardis who were true to Christ, a threefold promise was given.

First, they would be dressed in white. In their Roman culture, this was significant, for they would have been reminded of the day of Roman triumph, when true Roman citizens donned the white toga and joined in a majestic triumphal procession. Christ reminded the believers in Sardis that they would walk one day in triumph with Christ. Next, He said that He would never blot out their names from the heavenly register and finally they would be acknowledged by

Christ before the Father and His angels. Those are lofty promises, and I can imagine some of those faithful ones reading and re-reading that letter eagerly, being sustained during times when it looked the darkest.

Have you ever been in a dead church? It is like going to a funeral, only many sitting in the cold pews don't realize that rigor mortis has set in.

A news story quoted the Reverend Daniel Weis comparing "mainline Protestantism to the Prophet Ezekiel's vision of a 'valley of dead, dry bones.'" He added that "these bones can live . . . through our transformation as a people revitalized by the Spirit."[9]

Philadelphia: The Missionary Church

Of all the churches, this is the one you may remember, because its name is familiar. If I had been a first-century man, the church at Philadelphia is where I would have liked to have my membership. In some ways, Philadelphia reminds me of where I live, in San Diego County, because it was frequently shaken by earthquakes. (However, that's not the reason I would have wanted to live there.)

Like Smyrna, Philadelphia had no word of condemnation. This church had right doctrine and right living going hand in hand. Where doctrine is present, without love, it is legalism; where love is present without doctrine, it is humanism.

God promised to open doors for this loving church, to give it an opportunity to reach out to a lost world. Christ was (and is) the great door-opener. This is an exciting, and reassuring thing to know, because it is God, the Holy Spirit, who prepares the hearts of men to receive the Good News—not our plans, tracts, crusades, or feeble witnessing. Sometimes we defeat our personal witness by plunging in unceremoniously through a closed door. I know, because in my youthful zeal I have done just that. If the door is shut, don't put your shoulder to it and try to break it down!

The Philadelphian church was commended because it had "little strength." This is contrary to our human thinking, for we think we must be men and women of steel and iron to get God's work accomplished. We may be part of the 20 percent in the church who run the Sunday school, lead the choir, head the committees, and give the money. When we know that God has said, "My grace is sufficient for you, for power is perfected in weakness" (2 Corinthians 12:9), we can be sustained. When we are depending on buildings, budgets, staffs, organizational plans, and outreach, under our own power, we might as well be a business organization, rather than a church.

When a church is truly a church of the open door to the leading of His Holy Spirit, then watch out world! It is not enough to have the truth or right doctrine. These will die if we don't go through the open door. Churches that have vibrant missions and believe God for great things will reach out to the world.

In church history, the period of great missionary outreach, from 1750 until around 1925, was exemplified by the Church of Philadelphia. This was the era of Hudson Taylor, John Wesley, George Whitfield, Charles Haddon Spurgeon, D. L. Moody, and many more. The Salvation Army was founded; a whole galaxy of home missionary agencies sprung up. It was a time of great spiritual awakening.

Prophetic Promises to Philadelphia—And to Us

Wonderful promises are made to this church, promises that are key to understanding prophecy. First, He promises that there is an open door for believers to reach out to a lost world. We don't have to be eloquent or slick, we just need to be prayerfully available to His leading. What a comforting thought for timid souls who love the Lord, but have not had a course in "how to lead someone to Christ."

Listen to this! It stirs me to the core to have the Lord promise: "Since you have kept my command to endure patiently, I will also keep you from the hour of trial that is going to come upon the world" (Revelation 3:10). The Lord has a special plan that will keep the Philadelphia church (and all true believers) from the world-wide tribulation which is to come!

The "hour of trial" is the Great Tribulation, which we will describe in later chapters. Notice He does not say, "I will keep you *through* the hour of trial," but *"from* the hour of trial." This refers to the Rapture, when Jesus will catch away God's people for Himself. We are pre-Tribulational in our beliefs, and we clearly see in this promise that the church will not go through the Tribulation. How can the clarity of this promise be explained any other way?

Notice that in chapters one through three of Revelation the church is mentioned nineteen times. After chapter four the Tribulation is described, but the church is not mentioned.

There are three positions on the Rapture, and we had better know what we believe or we will be shaken by every headline, every catastrophe, and every apostasy of our day. First, there is the pre-Tribulational view which says all true believers will be raptured before the Tribulation begins. Second, there is the view that the church will be raptured in the middle of the Tribulation, or as the Great Tribulation begins. Third, some believe we will live through the Tribulation and be raptured and go up with the Lord at the end.

I know of a man who was the pastor of a very large, evangelical church and on one occasion he said, "If I'm gone when the Tribulation begins, then I'm pre-Trib; if I stay around for three and a half years and then I'm raptured, I'm mid-Trib; if I live through the Tribulation, then I'm post-Trib. Whatever happens, I'm pan-Trib—everything will pan out all right."

While this may be humorous, unfortunately he is wrong, and he is denying his flock the assurance of the blessed hope.

An old Southern preacher said, "It's time for our church to wake up and sing up, preach up and pray up and never give up or let up or back up or shut up, until the church is filled up or we go up. Amen."

In every church today there are those who could have been members of the church in Ephesus, that had lost its first love or of Smyrna, the suffering ones. Modern members of Pergamum attend where Satan has his foothold. Thyatiran church-goers are weighted down with sexual sin while the Sardians are among the walking dead. The Philadelphians are filled with love. In fact, at different times we may possess the qualities of several of these churches.

As the historical time line of these churches approaches our era, there is a church which will be on earth when Christ returns. Is this the church of the latter part of the twentieth century? If so, it's later than we think.

5

THE LUKEWARM CHURCH IN THE LAST DAYS

What is the meaning of life? People with varied back-grounds were asked that question and one view was expressed by a taxi driver who said, "We're here to die, just live and die. Life is a big fake. Nobody gives a damn. You're rich or you're poor. You're here, you're gone. You're like the wind. After you're gone, other people will come. We're gonna destroy ourselves, nothing we can do about it. The only cure for the world's illness is nuclear war—wipe everything out and start over."[1]

Hopelessness is the saddest expression of man's feelings. Without hope we may exist, but we do not live.

The church should be the place where the present hope of Jesus Christ and the future hope of His return to establish His kingdom is proclaimed. Is this happening in every church today?

Within some churches who claim His name, are those

who say that Christ's kingdom can be established here on earth during His absence. This movement takes various names: kingdom, dominion, reconstruction. The basic premise is that mortal man can accomplish what only the immortal Lord can perform. They believe that society must be reconstructed by Christians to establish the kingdom of God on earth before the personal return of Jesus Christ. Although this is a simplification of all the views espoused by the exponents of dominion theology, I believe they are removing the fire from evangelicalism and replacing it with dying embers. Their understanding of end-time prophecies is lacking.

A leading exponent of kingdom (or dominion) theology says, ". . . the kingdoms of this world must be steadily transformed into the kingdom of Christ . . . this historical transfer of kingdom ownership to Christ is to be made manifest in history."[2]

Today there are many Christians who are bent on changing society through government programs, lobbying activities, civil disobedience, and pressure groups. I do not find any place in the Bible that says this is the mission of the church of Jesus Christ. The mission of the church is witnessing to lost souls about the redemption provided by the Lord Jesus Christ. This mission is being replaced by those who believe the kingdom of God can be established here and now by our human activities.

Jesus warned that in the last days before His return there would be a church which would brag about its growing strength and self-importance. Today there are many undiscerning Christians who are looking for the kingdom of God on earth, a kingdom where justice will reign and nations will exist in peaceful coexistence. This arrogant church covets political power, not the power of God. The revival we have sought seems so slow in coming, that many believe Christians should take over the reins of government and legislate righteousness. Even the halls of Congress echo with a pharisaic piety, demanding outward vows of morality from its members.

I've asked myself these hard questions: "Would the history

of nearly 2,000 years of the church of Jesus Christ have been changed if the martyrs during the era of the Roman caesars had overturned the despotic rulers? What would have happened in Babylon if Daniel had wrested the reins of government from Nebuchadnezzar? Would John have received and written the Revelation of Jesus Christ in a plush office in Laodicea, rather than the rocky desolation of Patmos? Are today's Christians convinced that placard-carrying, slogan-bearing demonstrators can replace soul-winners?"

There *is* a better world coming, but not until those left on earth experience a time of evil fiercer than this planet has ever seen.

As an American who believes our country is the greatest, I want to do everything I can to fight injustice, and I support political candidates whose views are closest to biblical truths. However, I am dismayed to see what has happened in our generation to draw the church away from its central task.

Another direction is being taken by some Christian leaders to join with cultists to form a coalition for what they call "Christian causes." One group of American clergymen joined with Sun Myung Moon, the man who claims to be the second Messiah, to lobby for political candidates. How can the witness of the church be strengthened by these activities?

I believe we must be wary of the associations we form and the causes we champion.

Richard Halverson, the esteemed chaplain of the U.S. Senate, said, "The more I listen to evangelicals talk, the less I hear about the hope of Christ's coming again and the more I hear about making the USA a Christian nation, a prosperous nation . . . sometimes I think if Christ would come back, it would constitute a terrible interruption of their plans."[3]

A Look Inside the Last Church on Earth

The final church mentioned in Revelation is the lukewarm church of Laodicea, the church which will be in existence when

Christ returns. I believe the majority of churches in these final days of the twentieth century are lukewarm. Let's look at the similarities between the organized Christian community today and the Laodicean church.

The church which received the last letter from the postman at Patmos was outwardly impressive. It had all the trappings of wealth, but something was missing.

Under Roman rule, the city of Laodicea had become widely known for its banking establishments, medical school, and textile industry. However, with all this affluence, the church had been lulled to sleep. The members were rich in material goods, but spiritually poor. The Lord had nothing positive to say about this church; in fact, it made Him sick. It's interesting that God looks at apostasy and gets angry—but He looks at indifference and becomes ill.

The preaching in the church was compromising. The pastor probably didn't want to upset his congregation. Maybe he rattled their consciences a little—just enough to bring out the guilt and fill the collection plate, but what he wanted to hear after the service was, "That was a wonderful sermon, pastor. I enjoyed it very much."

The Lord says, ". . . because you are lukewarm—neither hot nor cold—I am about to spit you out of my mouth" (Revelation 3:16).

This is the only place in the New Testament where the word "lukewarm" is used. The expression is drawn from the geography of the area that surrounded the city. In the district of Hierapolis were hot mineral springs, whose water was transported to Laodicea in conduits. By the time it reached the city, it was no longer hot. Cold water was piped to Laodicea from Colossae, and it, too, would be lukewarm by the time it arrived. Lukewarm is the same as allowing coffee to cool and lemonade to warm.

In the Bible there are three possible heart temperatures: the *burning heart:* ". . . were not our hearts burning within us while he talked with us on the road and opened the Scriptures to us?" (Luke 24:32); the *cold heart* "Because of the increase of wickedness, the love of most will grow cold" (Matthew 24:12), and the *lukewarm heart* of the last church.

John Stott wrote: "The Laodicean church was a half-hearted church. Perhaps none of the seven letters is more appropriate to the twentieth-century church than this. It describes vividly the respectable, sentimental, nominal, skin-deep religiosity which is so widespread among us today. Our Christianity is flabby and anemic. We appear to have taken a lukewarm bath of religion."[4]

We are so afraid of being on fire for Christ; we don't want to be labeled as fanatics or extremists, yet in every other area of life we shed our proper manners and exude enthusiasm. I've shouted myself hoarse at a football or basketball game, and clapped until my hands were red for a talented singer or musician. Emerson said that nothing great was ever achieved without enthusiasm, but much of our Christian experience is as limp as an overcooked noodle.

I remember hearing of an eccentric man who walked around town with a sandwich sign slung over his shoulders. The front of the sign said: "I am a fool for Christ's sake." As he strolled the streets, he was ridiculed by those who saw the front of his placard, until he walked by and they read what was written on the back: "Whose fool are you?"

The lukewarm Laodicean church was conceited: "You say, 'I am rich; I have acquired wealth and do not need a thing.' But you do not realize that you are wretched, pitiful, poor, blind and naked" (Revelation 3:17).

The wealthy banking city had squeezed the church into its mold; the spirit of the marketplace had crept in and values became twisted. The church was proud of its ministry because it used the human measuring standard, instead of the divine.

David Wilkerson, author of *The Cross and the Switchblade,* commented: "Jesus clearly warned that a church would evolve in the last days of civilization which would boast that it was rich, growing, increasing in numbers, and self-sufficient.

. . . For nearly two thousand years the church of Jesus Christ has been rejected and persecuted by the world. The blood of millions of rejected martyrs cries out from the ground. The Bible says they all died in faith and the world was not worthy of them. Am I now to believe that Jesus has changed his mind and has decided to close out the ages with a lukewarm, rich, pampered, boastful, self-centered church? Will the last army of God consist of precinct workers getting out the vote? Will the soul-winners be replaced with petitioners going into the highways and hedges seeking signatures for some social cause?"[5]

The Great Physician's Prescription for a Sick Body

Some people think they don't need a doctor. "I can take care of myself, nobody needs to tell me what to do," boasts the self-sufficient man. Then comes the gripping pain in the chest, a shortness of breath, and the gasping plea, "Call a doctor!" The fellow recovers, but not until a physician gives him some strong admonitions about a change in lifestyle.

Christ gave us specific prescriptions for the sick church of the end times. He wrote them out clearly, so that anyone could read the directions. First He said, "Those whom I love I rebuke and discipline. So be earnest, and repent" (Revelation 3:19).

Notice that He didn't say, "Think about it," or "When you get around to it," but do it now! The weakness of compromise must be replaced by the humility of repentance.

Another prescription was given for the church's spiritual poverty. He told the people they must no longer trust in their banks, but come to Christ for His riches. The Laodiceans were well endowed with the riches of this earth, but what they really needed they could not buy with their gold.

If a person walked down the street stark naked, he would be arrested and carted off to jail or a mental institution. The Laodiceans were like the emperor in Hans Christian Andersen's story; they thought they were clothed in splendor, when they were really naked! Christ wanted to clothe them in "white clothes to wear, so you can cover your shameful nakedness" (Revelation 3:18).

The idea of spiritual nakedness in the Bible refers to being spiritually defeated and humiliated. White clothes (or fine linen, clean and white) symbolize the righteous acts of believers. The lukewarm lifestyle of the Laodicean church needed to be transformed into a lifestyle of red hot zeal for God.

The next prescription was for the cure of spiritual blindness. Revelation 3:18 refers to "salve to put on your eyes, so you can see."

In the city of Laodicea there was a medical school. One of the medicinal products manufactured and exported from that medical center was a tablet that was sold all over the Roman Empire. This tablet was used to heal a wide range of eye ailments: the instructions said to crush the tablet, mix it with a small amount of water, rub it on the eyes, and wait for the healing. Jesus reminded the blind Laodiceans that they needed more than their precious eye salve to see; they needed the truth of God which only Christ could bring to them.

It makes me think of the spiritual blindness of New Agers and Reconstructionists, whose vision is so sadly blinded, or the church-goers who "enjoy" the sermon and the music, and leave without any change of heart.

The final prescription is a positive cure for compromise, poverty, nakedness, and blindness. The greatest invitation in the Bible is contained in Revelation 3:20:

"Here I am! I stand at the door and knock. If anyone hears my voice and opens the door, I will come in and eat with him, and he with me."

When Jesus came the first time He was not received by His own people (John 1:11). During His first visit to this planet, Christ predicted that His second coming would also be met with unbelief (Luke 18:8).

The condition of the church at the time of Christ's return is Christless. Notice He says, "if *anyone* hears my voice . . . I will come in." While the hierarchy in many end-time churches has denied Christ entrance to their organizations, He still knocks at the door of each person's heart.

God does not force Himself upon anyone. No one is saved against his will; no one is compelled to obedience who wants to be rebellious. Notice that this invitation is extended to the last church ever mentioned in the Bible. That fact grips me with urgency for our day.

G. Campbell Morgan said: "The only cure for lukewarmness is the readmission of the excluded Christ. Apostasy must be confronted with His fidelity, looseness with conviction born of His authority, poverty with the fact of His wealth, frost with the mighty fire of His enthusiasm, and death with the life divine that is in His gift. There is no other cure for the malady of the world, for the lukewarmness of the Church than the readmitted Christ."[6]

The Church at the Crossroads

Seven churches have been described in this last book of the Bible. In our present age we may have difficulty seeing ourselves as belonging to any of these churches; however, some of their characteristics are found in each one of us.

The church at Ephesus was once strong, but it had lost its first love. It had become lifeless, forgetting the passion and excitement of its original love for Jesus.

The church at Smyrna was a suffering church, enduring hardship for its faith.

The church at Pergamum had fallen under the influence of the pagan culture in which it lived.

The church at Thyatira had become part of an evil cult.

The Sardian church was so cold and dead that only the names in the church directory could have indicated any living members.

The church in Philadelphia was a loving church, the one for which the Lord had no negative words.

Finally, we have visited the weak, lukewarm church of Laodicea.

Why are there no more letters to other churches? What happened to the church of Jesus Christ after the Laodicean era? Did it disappear?

If we are living in that time of the last church on earth before Christ's return, what other signs are pointing toward that cataclysmic event?

The hour hand on God's time clock is wound up and spinning. We are being swept along the path of history by a swift wind at our backs. Our individual ability to weather the storm will come from our understanding of the Word of God. We need only heed what has echoed through the centuries: "He who has an ear, let him hear what the Spirit says to the churches" (Revelation 3:22).

6

EARTH'S RACE TO THE FINISH

When Noah started building that weird-looking boat on dry land, his neighbors probably laughed and said, "This guy is really a pessimist."

Jeremiah warned the people of Judah that unless they quit their evil lifestyle the country would fall to Nebuchadnezzar's army, but Jeremiah was tied in stocks, thrown in jail, and tossed down a well. Pessimism does not make one popular.

In the time of Israel's kings there was a fellow named Micaiah, who told King Ahab he would be killed in a battle against the Syrians. Micaiah was hated for his gloomy prophecy.

Were these men positive or negative thinkers? The flood came, Babylon conquered Judah, Micaiah got an arrow through his heart. Pessimism and optimism are irrelevant in every situation where God's Word is given.

The Bible warns, but provides a way of escape. Men also warn us, but offer only human methods of coping in a world under crisis management. In earth's race to a finish, we

66

are provided with God's view and bombarded with man's solutions.

The Things Which Are

When Jesus told John to "Write, therefore, what you have seen, what is now and what will take place later" (Revelation 1:19), He gave us the panorama of history. Today, living in the Laodicean age of the last church, we are in the time before Christ will come again. All the signs are pointing in the same direction, only man is attempting to devise a detour.

Remember John was an old man, exiled to a lonely island in the Aegean, when Christ appeared to him in His resurrected, glorified body. John was so shaken that he fainted, just as Daniel did when the angel Gabriel appeared to him and prophesied to him of the end times. Both men took these prophecies seriously, and so should we.

When John regained consciousness, Jesus told him the reason for His visit. John was to be the person who would see God's future for mankind, and he was to write so that everyone could read and be able to interpret it in the light of current events. John was told to record three things: first, what he had seen in the glorified Christ; second, the spiritual conditions of the seven churches—churches that would exemplify attitudes and actions of people and congregations throughout the ages; and third, the events of the end of this world as we know it, and the certainty of a new world coming.

The old prisoner of Patmos was well chosen for his awesome task. More than sixty years before he recorded Revelation, John, a first cousin to Jesus and one of the inner circle, was a member of the little band of disciples who hovered around their Master on the Mount of Olives. It was the last week before the Crucifixion, and Christ had many things to tell His followers; future happenings mystified them. One of the disciples, and it might have been John, asked, "What will be the sign of Your coming and of the end of the age?"

Jesus didn't give them just one sign, but several. When we read His words in Matthew 24, the headlines become bolder, they roll across the screen of our mind as if we're viewing some heavenly edition of the *Prophetic Daily News.*

New Age—Old Prophecy

Jesus warned, "For many will come in my name, claiming, 'I am the Christ,' and will deceive many" (Matthew 24:5).

Deception is rampant in the world system today, so that even believers can be caught in its snare. First, let's look at some of the more blatant forms.

Sometimes it is a person who develops a following by claiming some sort of "spiritual inner awareness," or Christlike powers. One man who called himself John-Roger—and the hyphenated name is a planned affectation—drew a large group of disciples who believed he was the embodiment of a Christlike power called the "Mystic Traveler Consciousness." He claimed to have left the earth after an operation in 1962, and a spiritual entity entered his body who was "John the Beloved." From that time on Roger D. Hinkins became John-Roger, the founder of an organization called "Insight."[1]

Christ impostors abound in our time. They don't all claim the name of Jesus, but call themselves by many names. Gurus and swamis are not always garbed in saris, distributing flowers to the faithful. They come in respectable guises, advocating such honorable-sounding phrases as "Christ-consciousness," "universal Oneness," "the divine within," "transpersonal psychology," "human potential," "holistic health," ad infinitum. When Jesus warned that "many shall come in my name," He described the basis for what is called the "New Age" movement today.

The New Age movement has such a shifting perspective that the central issue one day may change the next. It is like the "winds of doctrine" Paul warns about in his letter to the

Ephesians (4:4). The basic theme, however, can be discerned whenever we see man glorified as the designer and maker of his own destiny, instead of depending upon God's sovereignty. Secular humanism and New Age thinking are fraternal twins.

To the New Ager, God is an impersonal energy, force, or consciousness. We see exciting, award-winning movies, such as *Star Wars,* and are caught in idolizing the power of the "Force." God is not portrayed as Someone with whom we may have a personal relationship, but as an extraterrestrial, benign being.

The New Age and its aberrations claim we are all gods, we have a universal goodness. The best-selling author of *The Color Purple,* Alice Walker, is quoted as saying that she is one with the universe, and "Once you feel loved by the universe, you're already accepted and you're not really concerned about offending people."[2]

Shirley MacLaine, the actress-turned-spiritual authority, claims that her book *Out on a Limb* was indirectly inspired by an extraterrestrial named "the Mayan."

We need to be enlightened, to experience disciplined meditation or other consciousness-raising techniques in order to understand ourselves, our surroundings, and experience inner peace, according to New Age thinking. "There are many names for this transforming experience: cosmic consciousness, God-realization, self-realization, enlightenment, illumination, Nirvana (Buddhist), stori (Zen), at-one-ment or satchitananada (Hindu)."[3]

New Agers see all religions as one; there are many paths to God and truth, but the common bond is "the god within." In his well-researched book, *Unmasking the New Age,* Douglas Groothuis said "Jesus of Nazareth, then, is no longer said to be the only begotten Son of God, the God-man, the Lord and Savior of the cosmos. He is merely one of many appearances or manifestations of God throughout the millennia . . . . The Christ of the Bible is redefined and made the ventriloquist's puppet for the New Age. Christ as the mediator between God and humanity is replaced with the idea of 'Christ-consciousness'. . . ."[4]

When Jesus warned His followers of the signs of the end of the age, He foresaw the burgeoning New Age movement. It is extending its tentacles into many aspects of our society.

Wars, Famines, Pestilences, and Earthquakes

"You will hear of wars and rumors of wars, but see to it that you are not alarmed. Such things must happen, but the end is still to come. Nation will rise against nation, and kingdom against kingdom. There will be famines and earthquakes in various places. All these are the beginning of birth pains" (Matthew 24:6–8).

Jesus told His little band of disciples that in the last days before He returned, labor pains like those before childbirth would increase before the birth of a new world. Let's count the frequency and intensity of these pains.

Wars and Rumors

Where will the guns sound next? We have become news-immune, as we are inoculated every day with the headlines from countries that only yesterday were different colors in our junior high school geography books. Wars and rumors of wars are a part of our daily routine, exploding as the citizens of the world step on another land mine planted by some despot. The aspect of a final holocaust lurks in the subconscious mentality.

The years pass and the world has not experienced a devastating nuclear disaster; the black death of Hiroshima has faded into the gray smog of the present. Countries once locked behind dictatorships are emerging from oppression to freedom. Even the specter of war begins to dim in contrast to the erosion of natural resources; economic and political futurists are sounding a new alarm for the human race. Extinction, they say, may not be with explosion, but through erosion.

Faces of Famine

Rivet your eyes on the images of starving people; I am moved to tears as I view the pathetic need for mere survival rations in many of the Third World countries. As we pour resources into some of these regions, it's like adding a cup of water to an ocean of starving humanity. Thank God there are organizations like World Vision, Samaritan's Purse, and Food for the Hungry that are showing the love of Christ in a tangible way to millions of the world's hungry. God's people must not stand by and watch His helpless ones starve without offering help. However, the prognosis for the survival of many is very poor.

The Worldwatch Institute is an organization of many scientists and researchers that publishes an annual *State of the World* report. The views of these scholars are significant in light of Bible prophecy, although this is not their stated purpose. Listen to what they are saying: "No generation in the past has faced the prospect of mass extinction within its lifetime," writes environmental consultant Norman Myers. "The problem has never existed before. No generation in the future will ever face a similar challenge: if this present generation fails to get to grips with the task, the damage will have been done and there will be no 'second try.'"[5]

"The earth is again poised on the brink of a global extinction crisis. This one, however, is being set in motion by human activities. The human population, now over 5 billion, is expected to nearly double in the next four decades. Worse, most of the expansion to 10 billion and beyond will occur in developing countries, where human poverty and biological wealth seem locked in a tragic embrace."[6]

We may travel through America, marveling that there are still vast, undeveloped areas in our land, but throughout the world swarms of people are running out of space and food. *Time* magazine reserved its 1989 cover issue, usually given to the Man or Woman of the Year, to an old friend on the critical list, the "Planet of the Year," subtitled "Endangered

Earth." Famine was featured: "In the poorest countries, growth rates are outstripping the national ability to provide the bare necessities. . . . In India, according to government reports, 37 percent of the people cannot buy enough food to sustain themselves."[7]

Man may have some influence over the advance of wars and famines, but only God controls the weather. Now we are being warned of another onslaught, called "the Greenhouse Effect." We are told that the worldwide warming which threatens to raise the earth's temperature considerably by the year 2050 is "generating some of the most difficult questions political leaders have ever had to deal with . . . If the world stays on the current path, crises will compound and accelerate until they overwhelm the capacity of institutions to respond. Time is of the essence."[8]

Red lights are flashing from every think tank in the world. Leaders of the Worldwatch Institute are saying, "Today, most of the battles to protect the planet's health are being lost."[9]

If I didn't know the Lord, and if I hadn't read the end of the book, I would be in despair at this point. How are the concerned citizens of the world keeping their sanity in the light of these ominous signs? Perhaps most of them don't want to face reality, so they revert to the old ostrich syndrome.

Have the pundits come up with any answers? Yes, they have, and one of their predominant solutions will be described later.

Pestilences

Pestilences were listed by Jesus as signs of His coming again. During epidemics in the past, such as the bubonic plague, great portions of mankind were affected. However, there has never been a world-wide, on-going plague like the one we are experiencing today. The multiplying horror of AIDS is another phenomenon of this age.

Dr. Harvey Fineberg, dean of the Harvard School of Public Health, wrote, "AIDS is a modern affliction. The AIDS epidemic was fomented by changes in social mores and lifestyle that are unique to the latter part of the 20th century."[10]

I believe AIDS could be the pestilence Jesus described in the Olivet discourse (Matthew 24:7, KJV).

Since 1981, when AIDS was recognized, it has become an international issue. Because its latency period is eight years or longer, thousands of people will never know they are infected with the virus until the body's immune system is gradually undermined. It is spreading faster than crabgrass in an untended lawn.

The scientific community is saying, "The AIDS epidemic exposes hidden vulnerabilities in the human condition."[11]

When we see the Pale Horse of the Apocalypse, this epidemic will have more significance.

Earthquakes

Jesus said there would be an increase in earthquakes, and today seismographs are recording their frequency. For a period of more than 1,000 years, fifteen major earthquakes, claiming thousands of lives, were recorded. In the past fifty-four years, twenty-one major quakes have shaken the foundations of man's security. *Life* magazine reported that in the last fifteen years nearly 500,000 people have died in earthquakes—more than in any other type of natural disaster.[12]

The energy released by earthquakes may cause damage for thousands of miles. Quakes can generate huge ocean waves, such as the Alaska quake of 1964 that moved down the Pacific coast at speeds of more than 400 miles per hour, demolishing stores and drowning people as far away as Crescent City, California. In Armenia, the destruction was so widespread that the little country experienced its worst natural disaster in a millennium.

In California, the nagging question is, "When will the Big One hit?"

Scientists speculate, "Just when the next great earthquake will test the region remains undetermined. The common wisdom is that there is a better than 40% probability that the big one will strike within the next 30 years."[13]

I have no right to sit back complacently and say, "I have no control over these things, so there's nothing I can do." On the contrary, the encroaching darkness in our beautiful world motivates me to speak up and write that Christians have the only hope, and we must pour it out, pass it around, shout it to the world.

Love Will Grow Cold

Jesus said, "Because of the increase of wickedness, the love of most will grow cold, but he who stands firm to the end will be saved" (Matthew 24:12).

Do you remember when doors were left unlocked, children played on the city sidewalks until bedtime, home security alarms were faithful dogs, and you checked your luggage at the airport and walked straight to the departing gate? If any of those are just memories of a safer world, then you have seen in your lifetime, as I have, the appalling increase in lawlessness. What will the next generation experience, if the Lord delays His coming? Do you believe wickedness, once entrenched and growing, will decrease?

Minds cannot conceive what the next horror will be. Six teenagers assaulted a young woman in Central Park, New York, beat her senseless with a rock and metal pipe, raped her, and left her for dead. One boy was reported to be a "born-again Christian," and only one boy had ever been in trouble with the police. A new word sprang into the media: "wilding" was the identification given to the wanton actions of this gang of boys. *Time* magazine described this event as

". . . capturing with shocking force the latent fears of a troubled age."[14]

A Drugstore on Every Corner

When some of us were kids, a drugstore was a place to get a coke and meet the gang after school. Today, "coke" means "cocaine" to many young and older people.

In a world ruined by man, the drug picture is a startling fulfillment of the "increase of wickedness." How the heart of Jesus must break as He watches the children of our generation poisoning their bodies with alcohol and drugs, and killing themselves or others as a result. School crime is up to a point that one-third of 11,000 adolescents polled in 1988 said they had been threatened, robbed, or attacked at school. This study was based on written responses of eighth through tenth graders in more than 200 schools in twenty states.[15]

As evil increases in intensity, Christian influence is becoming weaker. In the last days, a lukewarm church limps its way through our modern culture. However, this sad commentary on lifeless churches is brightened when we see pockets of on-fire believers and churches who exemplify the love of Christ. Jesus gave His disciples some positive prophecy when He said, "And this gospel of the kingdom will be preached in the whole world as a testimony to all nations, and then the end will come" (Matthew 24:14).

The Lord does not want anyone to perish, for He is a loving God and His desire is to see everyone saved.

Can you imagine those twelve men, limited in their view of the world by their own small country, thinking, *How can the gospel be preached to the whole world? There are only twelve of us!* Fifty years ago do you think anyone could understand how this prophecy could be fulfilled? Twenty years ago? There weren't enough missionaries to penetrate the continents. But what is happening today?

Saturate with Satellites

Satellite technology is able to spread the gospel to every corner of the globe. One evangelist, Billy Graham, at the peak of his ministry, is preaching via satellite to millions around the world. During one crusade alone, twenty-three African countries were able to hear God's Word presented simultaneously in their own languages. What an exciting fulfillment of Jesus' words!

As we see Bible translators working on every known language, radios beaming gospel messages into remote corners, and now satellites, we can watch for more signs of the earth's race toward prophecy fulfillment.

Getting Smarter and Smarter (?)

"In the middle of the 20th century, it was estimated that the pace of change was as much as 50 times greater than the average pace in previous centuries."[16]

The prophet Daniel was told that in the last days knowledge would increase (Daniel 12:4). Will anyone who has lived longer than twenty years deny this fact? An electronics manufacturer said, "If it works, it's obsolete." Today, knowledge is increasing so fast that parents can't keep up with what their third-graders are learning. There is no such thing as the simple life; we are simply frazzled with the speed of modern living. The age of mega-knowledge is leaving many of us with the feeling that we're hanging on to the tail of the Concorde, heading for obsolescence.

It wasn't too long ago that I struggled with the complexities of a personal computer. After losing entire sermon notes, getting headaches from staring at the screen, and pushing the help button (but not understanding what the menu meant), I finally thought I had mastered the confounded machine. Now I'm told that my program is obsolete. Sometimes I think my brain has been put on hold and machines are taking over.

Take Me to Your Leader

Man is always devising solutions for drug use, crime, and immorality. We should continue to do so, but some of the answers for such concerns as pollution are leading into a vision of one world. The buzz words of the day are "global cooperation," and "international unity." In 1987 a report was released by the World Commission on Environment and Development which stated that we need to move "from one earth to one world."[17]

This prestigious group, comprised of leading members of the scientific, economic, and political community, are the Paul Reveres of the environment, shouting the warning that disaster is coming. "Species lost cannot be recreated. Soil washed away may take centuries, if not millennia, to replace even under careful husbandry. Once the earth gets warmer there will be no practical way of cooling it."[18]

Yes, the heat is on! The Worldwatch Institute Report says the remedy is to create new international institutions to promote responsible behavior. The same clarion call is being sounded from many sources. Isaac Asimov, one of the most prolific authors of our time, built his case for World Government on the environmental crisis: He wrote that the one hope was that fear of destruction would drive us together to work out "global solutions."[19]

In its cover story on the "Planet of the Year," *Time* magazine sounded the death knell for the environment, "Yet humanity is in a war right now, and it is not too Draconian to call it a war for survival . . . both the cause and effects of the problems that threaten the earth are global, and they must be attacked globally."[20]

Who will find the solution? "Mobilizing that sort of mass commitment will take extraordinary leadership, of the kind that has appeared before in times of crisis."[21]

A strong world leader, with a forceful, intelligent, charismatic personality, will rise on the scene, stepping in at the eleventh hour with plausible solutions. He will be granted power and authority, because he comes with such noble motives to fill a void in a vacuum of leadership. The world is preparing for his entrance now.

In the Days of Noah

Jesus told the disciples that before He returned the earth would be as it was "in the days of Noah." While Noah was building the ark on dry land, his neighbors were laughing at what they believed were the efforts of a madman. They really didn't care what that family of religious fanatics did, because their lives were so evil and self-centered that God's warnings were ignored. One of the most vivid descriptions of total depravity is found in Genesis 6:5: "The Lord saw how great man's wickedness on the earth had become, and that every inclination of the thoughts of his heart was only evil all the time."

In the days before the flood, people were looking out for number one, until that final hour when the Noah family and their animal friends entered the ark. When the flood came, the remaining citizens of earth had no dry ground or life rafts to rescue them. With their last drowning breaths, it was too late to ask God for mercy.

I Have Told You Ahead of Time

Jesus and His prophets told us all of the signs of His Second Coming. In the early 1970s Hal Lindsey wrote *The Late Great Planet Earth.* It chronicled the signs of the end times. Children have grown up since that book was written, and many of those signs have increased in such intensity that the warnings heard twenty years ago are now sounding like high-decibel sirens.

In the following chapters, there will be additional proof that tomorrow's events are casting their shadows on the world today. All systems are "go" for the greatest launching in the history of mankind. Clothed in the armor of God, His children are being gathered to the site of takeoff. The only question that remains is who is going to be on this world-wide space travel team.

Ten—nine—eight—seven—six—five—four—three—two—

Part III

THE WORLD TOMORROW:
Ruled by Satan

7

MILLIONS
MISSING

When I graduated from seminary I went to work as youth
director for a large New Jersey church. My assignment was
challenging, to say the least. Whenever you face a group of
teenagers, you're on trial. Are you current with their styles and
language? Will you be fun or stuffy? Do you know the latest
"in" words, or are you still saying "groovy"? I was told by the
senior pastor that my first contact with the young people
would be at a Summer Teen Conference, where I was expected
to teach a week-long study on Bible prophecy. Talk about a
trial by fire!

On the first night of the conference I asked a few kids to
play the roles of newsboys and hawk papers at the opening
session. They plunged into their parts with gusto and shouted
the headlines as they ran down the aisles:

"PEOPLE PANIC—MILLIONS MISSING
AROUND THE WORLD."

The lead article began:

At 12:05 last night a telephone operator reported three frantic calls regarding missing relatives. Within fifteen minutes all communications were jammed with similar inquiries. A spot check around the nation found the same situation in every city. Sobbing husbands sought information about the mysterious disappearance of wives. One husband reported, "I turned on the light to ask my wife if she remembered to set the clock, but she was gone. Her bedclothes were there, her watch was on the floor . . . she had vanished!"

An alarmed caller from Brooklyn tearfully reported, "My husband just returned from the late shift . . . I kissed him . . . he just disappeared in my arms."

Another feature read:

"THRONGS IN THE NATION DIE OF HEART ATTACK."

It began:

Thousands of coronary victims have died since the news was released concerning the multitudes who are missing. In Chicago the famed loop was the scene of multiple heart-attack victims. Fifty-five bodies were taken to the morgue for identification. In Los Angeles and New York it was reported that as many as 300 deaths from heart failure per hour are being called in to the hospitals.

The newspapers and television will not be able to report the magnitude of this news. Some will say this must be "The Rapture," because they heard about it in church or read about it in a book. Others will attempt to explain it scientifically, but will stumble over their own inadequacies.

The event described in our fictional newspaper (and, incidentally, it grabbed the attention of those kids) is the next on the prophetic calendar. It is not specifically mentioned in Revelation, but it is clearly indicated in the fourth chapter. There is only one explanation for the shift in emphasis from chapter three to chapter four, and that is that the Church has been raptured, the Christians are no longer on earth.

Events Clearly Outlined

"After this I looked, and there before me was a door standing open in heaven. And the voice I had first heard speaking to me like a trumpet said, 'Come up here, and I will show you what must take place after this'" (Revelation 4:1).

John was summoned to have a look into heaven, although he was still the old prisoner on earth; he saw and recorded a preview of coming attractions. He had finished writing his letter to Laodicea, but after that the church is never mentioned. Seven times in chapters two and three, we read, "He who has an ear, let him hear what the Spirit says to the churches." Then we read, "He who has an ear, let him hear" (Revelation 13:9). The Spirit is missing and the church is missing. They are obviously in heaven, while earth is suffering in the Tribulation.

Another interesting fact: the church's favorite name for God is "Father." From Revelation four until the end of chapter nineteen, God is not addressed as "Father": He is called God, Lord, Almighty, and other names by which He was known in the Old Testament.

Compare the "voice . . . like a trumpet" to other New Testament references. "For the Lord himself will descend from heaven with a shout, with the voice of the archangel, and with the trump of God . . ." (1 Thessalonians 4:16, KJV).

When Jesus Christ returns for His own, the world will not hear the voice nor the trumpet. The ears of the nonbelievers will be deaf and their eyes blind. It will take place so fast, "in the twinkling of an eye," that no one left on earth will understand what has happened.

John wrote that he was "in the Spirit" immediately, which means that he was transformed in shape and structure into another dimension. He was sent through nineteen hundred (or more) years of time and set down in heaven where he watched and recorded the horror of the Tribulation and the ultimate triumph of the Second Coming. What a view he had!

Open Door into Heaven

In Revelation 3 we saw a door closed and Christ was seeking entrance; now in chapter four we see an open door through which we can view the regal splendor of our God. Revelation four leads us into a throne room, where the King is sitting.

Twice in the book of Revelation we see an open door. The first time is in Revelation 4:1 when John sees "a door standing open in heaven," and the last time is in Revelation 19:11 when he "saw heaven standing open and there before me was a white horse." The first time the door opens, somebody goes up, and the next time, somebody comes down.

How can anyone describe God? Some people have said they have seen a "bright light" or felt a "presence." He has been pictured as a majestic old man with a long beard—a voice echoing across mountain walls—even George Burns descending through the clouds with a cigar in his mouth.

John likened Him to a precious stone, which the first readers of Revelation, converted Jews, could understand. The one on the throne had ". . . the appearance of jasper and carnelian" (4:3) which every informed Hebrew knew were the first and last stones in the breastplate of the high priest. Jasper is a clear gem, like our diamond: God's glory is more perfect than any gem Tiffany displays. Carnelian, or red sardius, is comparable to the ruby.

Encircling the throne, John saw a complete rainbow, a reminder that in heaven all things are complete; this emerald rainbow symbolizes life, and the circle indicates eternity.

After Christians are raptured, all the attention in heaven during Phase One of His coming will be upon the throne. God the Father is seated on the throne, and God the Son is standing before Him (Revelation 5:6).

Twenty-Four Elders, Our Personal Representatives

"Surrounding the throne were twenty-four other thrones, and seated on them were twenty-four elders" (Revelation 4:4).

I believe these elders represent the church in the same way the twenty-four elders of the Old Testament represented the entire body of priests.

The elders are dressed in white and have crowns upon their heads. These elders comprise the leaders of our heavenly delegation, but the crowns they wear are available to each of us. We may not be able to imagine ourselves wearing crowns, but, nevertheless, as children of the King we are heirs and heiresses of His riches.

There are five different crowns available as rewards for believers. It is conceivable that we might receive more than one!

The Crown of Incorruption is given to those who live a disciplined life. Competing in this game of life means that winners "do not run like a man running aimlessly" (1 Corinthians 9:26), but have a purpose, a goal in life.

The Crown of Life is given to those who with patience endure trials. James 1:12 says, "Blessed is the man who perseveres under trial, because when he has stood the test, he will receive the crown of life."

The Crown of Rejoicing is given to those who joyously expressed their faith (1 Thessalonians 2:19, 20). The joy of leading a person to Christ is only exceeded by knowing Him ourselves. What a sparkling crown will sit upon the head of the soul-winner!

The Crown of Glory is given to those who are faithful in ministering the Word. If I didn't believe the Bible to be true, I don't see how I could expect to be worthy of such a crown. The apostle Peter gave us these guidelines:

"To the elders among you, I appeal as a fellow elder, a witness of Christ's sufferings and one who also will share in the glory to be revealed: Be shepherds of God's flock that is under your care, serving as overseers—not because you must, but because you are willing, as God wants you to be; not greedy for money, but eager to serve; not lording it over those entrusted to you, but being examples to the flock. And when the Chief Shepherd appears, you will receive *the crown of glory* that will never fade away" (1 Peter 5:1–4, emphasis added).

The Crown of Righteousness is given to those who love His appearing, who are eagerly waiting for the return of Christ. How wonderful it would be to receive this crown. Jesus Christ is waiting to make His appearance, and that is exciting (2 Timothy 4:8)!

What a scene in heaven! Before the throne is a sea of glass, separating all other creatures, except the angels, from the glory of God. From the throne come flashes of lightning, voices, and peals of thunder. Judgment is about to fall on earth, the warnings are being heard. Center stage, around the throne, are four living creatures who, I believe, represent angels who are involved in worshiping God and carrying out His judgments on the world.

The twenty-four elders, hearing the voices of the angels, fall down upon their faces, casting their gold crowns at His feet. The whole scene is one beyond description. When John saw that vision, the Lord said, "Write it down, John."

The Judgment Seat

When we become believers in Jesus Christ, our sins, past, present, and future, have been judged at the Cross. "Therefore, there is now no condemnation for those who are in Christ Jesus . . ." (Romans 8:1). However, there is a time to come, after the dead in Christ have been raised, and those who remain are caught up in the air during the Rapture, when all of us will have our works on earth judged. God's people will be tested, not for the quantity of our works, but for their quality. It is then that we will receive our crowns to lay at the Savior's feet.

"Just get me in, that's good enough for me," is the unexpressed attitude of many believers. It is evident in the winter of the twentieth century that the lives of many Christians are cold. The rewards in this present life seem more appealing than eternal rewards. More money, more recognition, more experiences are sought for that elusive quality called "fulfillment." Of course, there are rewards in this life, but too many of us are storing up so many treasures on earth that we have no time for storing treasures in heaven.

Malcolm Muggeridge writes in *A Twentieth-Century Testimony:* "When I look back on my life nowadays, which I sometimes do, what strikes me most forcibly about it is that what seemed at the time most significant and seductive, seems now most futile and absurd. For instance, success in all of its various guises; being known and being praised; ostensible pleasures, like acquiring money or traveling, going to and fro in the world and up and down in it like Satan, explaining and experiencing whatever Vanity Fair has to offer.

"In retrospect, all these exercises in self-gratification seem pure fantasy, what Pascal called, 'licking the earth.'"[1]

In the Greek games, there was a seat where the judge sat and could see everything from start to finish; nothing was in the way to obstruct his view. When we stand before the Supreme Judge, He will be able to see all of our lives.

The judgment seat will be a time of truth for each of us. During our lifetime, we are all required to make judgments. What job will we take? What house should we buy? Whom should we marry? We try to make good judgments, but as one wit said, "Do you know how I get good judgment? By making bad judgments."

When Christ makes His judgments, there will be no missing information. Everything will be naked and open. The time of unmasking will ". . . bring to light what is hidden in darkness and will expose the motives of men's hearts" (1 Corinthians 4:5). We'll be in for some real surprises, too. Prominent men and women, recognized by the world for their philanthropies, but shallow in their commitment to Christ, will take a back seat to others who toiled behind the scenes, only desiring to do God's work.

Have you ever heard "there will be no more tears in heaven"? When we stand in front of Him, I believe there will be tears. Leap ahead with me to the end of Revelation, after the tribulation and at the end of the millennium. The kingdom of God will be established and *then* "He will wipe every tear from their eyes. There will be no more death or mourning or crying or pain . . ." (Revelation 21:4). Doesn't this infer that there will be tears before that time?

Yes, tears may flow because of opportunities neglected on earth, gifts left unused. We are provided with so many doorways to serve the Lord, but sometimes we're just too busy, or overburdened with our own problems. Tears will be shed over bad investments; some wealthy Christians have squandered their money on themselves while churches flounder, missionaries cannot be sent out, and the needs of others are ignored. Someday we may hear, "Why didn't you invest in eternal values?"

Tears will be shed because of neglected holiness. Many Christians are so dirtied by the world that one would never know they were Christians. It pains me to see professed believers living together without being married, cheating in business, indulging in promiscuity. His "eyes like a blazing fire" will look into our eyes someday. Will He find purity or cesspools?

Tears will be shed because rewards which could have been earned will be lost. I believe the Bible shows we could live many years with a degree of purity and throw it all away in the end. "Watch out that you do not lose what you have worked for, but that you may be rewarded fully" (2 John 8).

We have known too many men and women who have served God faithfully all their lives, and then in the last few years wiped it all out because of immorality and carnality. This is far too common in the Christian church. None of us is safe from the temptations of the world, but we all need to ask God to keep us true to the very end.

The judgment seat of Christ will be a time of terror. When the works Christians have done in the flesh, not in the power of the Holy Spirit, are revealed, it will be devastating. Some will see their life's work go up in smoke right before their eyes. "If what he has built survives, he will receive his reward. If it is burned up, he will suffer loss; he himself will be saved, but only as one escaping through the flames" (1 Corinthians 3:14, 15).

John adds to this by saying that some who will stand before the Lord in that day will be literally "ashamed" (1 John 2:28).

While we have taken the sting out of the judgment seat of Christ in much of our teaching and preaching, the Bible doesn't hide the fact that this, indeed, may be a time of terror for many believers.

The judgment seat is also a place of triumph. There will be rewards for those who have been steadfast, willing to serve. The quiet saint who prays is just as important as the public servant who preaches. God knows when a man preaches with the power of God that there is a host of people praying for him. For every man in the ministry who teaches God's Word, there's usually a wife praying for him, encouraging him.

A great reward will be given to those who have been persecuted for the sake of Christ. "Rejoice and be glad, because great is your reward in heaven, for in the same way they persecuted the prophets who were before you" (Matthew 5:12). Some of us feel we are persecuted when another person says something derogatory about us, or mocks us for our faith. We know very little of persecution in America, but if it should come, we have this promise to claim.

Every one of the writers of the New Testament was horribly persecuted: Matthew was beheaded, Mark was dragged through the streets of Alexandria by a team of wild horses until he died; Luke was hanged in an olive tree; John was thrown into a boiling cauldron of oil and survived, but was disfigured for life. One extrabiblical legend grew from this occurrence, which said that John saw his reflection in a river and was shocked by his own face; it was then God told him to write ". . . we know that when he appears, we shall be like him . . ." (1 John 3:2). Paul was beheaded; Peter and Jude were crucified; James was battered to death with a club. They didn't have elaborate funerals with satin-lined caskets, but the rewards of those who suffer for His name's sake will surpass the twenty-one-gun salute given for fallen heroes.

How Will We Run the Race?

A Christian youth was killed in a plane crash at the age of eighteen. Prominently displayed in his parents' home is a picture of him running in a high school track meet and inscribed on that photo are these words: "I have fought the good fight, I have finished the race, I have kept the faith. Now there is in store for me the crown of righteousness, which the Lord, the righteous judge, will award to me on that day" (2 Timothy 4:7, 8).

What awards will we get "on that day?" Will the judgment seat of Christ be a place for blue ribbons and gold medals, or will it be the site of humiliation?

Torture to Triumph

Crowns are reserved for God's faithful servants, like Adoniram Judson, a missionary who served in Burma. He was arrested and falsely accused of being an enemy agent. Imprisoned in a tiny cell, he was forced to stand so others could lie down and sleep. The sun was unbearably hot, and since they were not allowed to bathe, the stench was horrible. One day the officials decided prison was not enough punishment for this infidel, so they hoisted Judson into the air by his thumbs—pain filled every fiber of his body. When he was returned to his cell, his precious wife, Anne, would creep in after dark and whisper to him, "Hang on, Adoniram, God will give us the victory."

Week after tortuous week, Anne would come by every night to encourage him with the same words, "Hang on, Adoniram, God will give us the victory." One night she didn't come, and another night passed without a sign of her returning. Weeks went by and his loneliness grew to an unbearable level. No one told him that Anne was dying.

Months later, he was released, a man whose body was so broken it was a miracle he could walk. He began his search for his beloved wife, returning to the place where they used to live. As he limped toward his home, he saw a child sitting in the dirt, a little girl so covered with filth that he failed to recognize her as his own daughter. He picked her up and staggered into the tent, his eyes squinting through the darkness. It was then he saw her, a bundle of bones and rags lying on a cot, so weak and frail that she looked like a skeleton. It was his Anne, her beautiful hair fallen out and her bright blue eyes staring blankly at nothing. Hugging his daughter to his chest, he knelt down and wept, calling her name over and over—"Anne, Anne, O my darling Anne." His hot tears fell on her face and slowly her eyes began to move with recognition. She struggled to speak and her last words were, "Hang on, Adoniram, God will give us the victory."

That day Adoniram Judson lost his sweetheart, but not his faith. He lost his loved one, but not his courage. He began to preach again, and soon was building churches. When he died he left scores of churches and hundreds of Christian converts in that Muslim nation. He had fought the good fight, finished the race, and kept the faith, and will receive a crown of righteousness "on that day."

Reward or Rubble?

When I told that story at our church my voice was so choked I could scarcely continue. I was touched, not only by the strength of love between those two people, but also by the realization that living by faith in God is not just lip service. Some professing Christians run the rat race of life, searching for the next thrill, the new toy, the increased experience. Someday we are going to stand before God and be asked, "What did you do with the gifts I gave you?" Will we have rewards or rubble, tears or triumph?

It's never too late to make a change. We can start to live for Jesus Christ today, and have eternity's awards forever. As Corrie ten Boom used to say in her thick Dutch accent, her eyes twinkling with excitement, "The best is yet to be! Hallelujah!"

The best does not apply to the earthlings left behind. Without a Christian working in any office, teaching in any school, preaching in any church, contributing to any charity, what will the world be like? The Bible tells us, and it doesn't take a theologian to understand it. Our present earth is approaching the night and the appearance of a new world leader, a man described as the Dark Prince. He could be alive today.

8

FOUR RIDERS ON THE HORIZON

Turmoil reigns on earth. People wander through vacant rooms, looking for loved ones. The only churches that could offer any solace are empty. Ethical standards are replaced by vague value systems and truth is relative.

After the mass disappearing act of millions, those who remain will be tense, wondering what will happen next in this time of uncertainty. Some may cry, "God, where are You?"

God is on His throne in heaven. In His right hand He has a record of the sequence of events for the next seven years. The Father is holding a scroll with writing on both sides, containing seven seals which will reveal the sobering judgments to come upon the world before Jesus returns to earth.

Only One is worthy to take the scroll and reveal its contents, and that is the Lion of the tribe of Judah, the Root of David, the Lamb.

John, his old eyes filled with tears, watches while Jesus takes the scroll from His Father, and breaks the first seal. The four living creatures and the twenty-four elders are so overcome that they fall down to worship. Then heaven echoes with a new song:

> You are worthy to take the scroll
> and to open its seals,
> because you were slain,
> and with your blood you
> purchased men for God
> from every tribe and language and
> people and nation.
> You have made them to be a kingdom
> and priests to serve our God,
> and they will reign on the earth
> (Revelation 5:9).

As the scroll unrolls, one seal is removed to disclose the first in a series of judgments. When successive seals are removed, the scroll unrolls again, each time revealing a worse horror. Altogether, there are three series of judgments: the seven seals, seven trumpets, and seven bowls.

When the first seal is removed, John sees one of the infamous four horsemen of the Apocalypse.

Dark Prince on a White Horse

"I looked and there before me was a white horse! Its rider held a bow, and he was given a crown, and he rode out as a conqueror bent on conquest" (Revelation 6:2).

Astride his prancing stallion, the dark prince enters the world scene with a flashing smile and an air of confidence. He chooses a white horse, the symbol of a conqueror in oriental imagery, for his grand entrance.

At the beginning of the Tribulation, the dark prince enters as a victorious leader. There are two riders on white horses in Revelation: the first is this man, with a bow in his hand and a victor's crown on his head; the second is another man, with a sword for His weapon and a kingly crown upon his head. These two horsemen are diametrically different.

Donald Grey Barnhouse wrote this about them:

The counterfeit is revealed by a detailed comparison of the two riders. The One whose name is the Word of God has on His head "many crowns." The symbol is of all royalty and majesty. The Greek word is diadem. The horseman of the first seal wears no diadem. The false crown is the stephanos. Its diamonds are paste. It is the shop girl adorned with jewelry from the ten-cent counter imitating the lady born and bred who wears the rich jewels of her inheritance. All is not gold that glitters. No amount of gaudy trappings can deceive the spiritual eye. Clothes do not make the man in spite of the proverb.[1]

The first rider has a useless weapon, like an evil Don Quixote, but the second rider carries a sharp sword with which He can strike down the nations.

The great counterfeiter is none other than the Antichrist, who rides into the world at the beginning of the tribulation period to bring peace in the midst of global turmoil. The great imitator, the cleverest mimic of all time, he will conquer without war.

The world is looking for a man on a white horse. Nations are churning. Revolutions are toppling governments. In this nuclear age, men live with the threat of international catastrophe. The final dictator, promising peace and prosperity, will be welcomed as the savior and hope of the world; he will command the military and mesmerize the masses. Governments will be united under his leadership and the people of the earth will sigh with relief, believing their future will be brighter.

Foreshadows of the Dark Prince

Hostages held captive for a length of time begin to relate favorably to their captors. It's like having your arm twisted behind your back, your bones about to crack, when suddenly the painful vise is released. Freed from your torture, you mutter, "Thank you, thank you."

Beginning the decade of the '90s, former world tyrants are making overtures of peace. Freedom-loving people, anxious to resolve conflicts and build secure societies, want to believe these conciliatory words and promises. For a time, cautious optimism grows around the globe.

In the past, prophecy students wondered how a new world order composed of all nations could include Russia. Or how a world filled with nuclear weapons, terrorists, and madmen could begin to cry "peace and safety." Watch how newscasts that frequently open with stories of war and destruction begin to report peace treaties, cease-fires, summit meetings, and tumbling walls.

By the time this book is published the headlines will change, but I believe that today we are being lulled into a security which could be more disastrous than that of Neville Chamberlain, who returned in 1938 from a meeting with Adolf Hitler and declared there would be peace in our time. We know that within a year the Germans invaded Poland and World War II began.

When a terrorist leader promises to reform, I would like to know the cause of that reformation. Wise Solomon said, "Truth stands the test of time; lies are soon exposed" (Proverbs 12:19, TLB).

Like the movie villain with a white-toothed smile and a hidden gun, the rider on the white horse will carry peace symbols in front of him and evil plans in his back pocket.

The dark prince will bring peace to one of the world's hot spots, the Middle East. With Israel surrounded by enemies, the person who could resolve these conflicts would achieve a diplomatic coup.

Daniel says there is a "prince that shall come," who will make a covenant with Israel to protect her from her enemies (Daniel 9:26, 27). What a hero he will be! This world-class strong man will have the support of so many nations that his help will not only be welcomed, it will be sought.

This deceiving horseman is no stranger in the world. He

used his flattering bribes in the Garden of Eden. He goaded Cain into murdering his brother. He invaded the minds of the children of Israel as they wandered in the wilderness, making them doubt that God would lead them into the Promised Land. In the universal war between good and evil, truth and falsehood, there is no truce. The dark prince is great at making promises; all he wants are our souls.

The rider on the white horse is sending his agents into every corner of the globe. He loves to infiltrate the church . . . he creeps into sermons and even writes Sunday school curricula! He divides congregations and forces church splits, enjoying every minute of the resulting heartache. He forces missionaries to leave the field in discouragement and entices ministers to forsake pulpits for higher paying jobs.

Today, as never before in the past two thousand years, the spirit of the Antichrist is invading our world and our sanctuaries. Before he became a prisoner, John warned us to "test the spirits to see whether they are from God." How are we supposed to know? Here's one standard: if a teacher says that Jesus Christ was God come in flesh, that teacher passes the test. However, "every spirit that does not acknowledge Jesus is not from God. This is the spirit of the antichrist, which you have heard is coming and now is already in the world" (1 John 4:2).

We should not attend church with the supercritical attitude of looking for heresy in every doctrine or sermon; however, we need to be discerning about what we hear and believe.

Before he makes his physical appearance on the world scene, the dark prince has sent his advance guard into our educational system. In the past few generations the biblical principles of right and wrong, good and evil, have been diluted into an educational pabulum of "values." In his penetrating look at modern American society, Allan Bloom wrote in *The Closing of the American Mind:* "The courses in 'value-clarification' springing up in schools are supposed to provide models for parents and get children to talk about abortion, sexism or the arms race, issues the significance of which they cannot possibly understand. . . . Such 'values' will inevitably change as public opinion changes."[2]

If values are not absolute, how does anyone discover the difference between good and evil? Bloom asked students about evil and said, "They have no idea of evil; they doubt its existence."[3]

Precursors of the dark prince are the deceivers within us who say we can sin and get away with it. Cheat a little here, lie a bit there, tear down another's reputation by innuendo, no one will know. The Bible tells us we will reap what we sow. It's those "invisible" sins that are so deceptive. We are not immune to deception, even when we go to Bible-believing churches, read Christian books (or write them), or attend a Bible study once a week. We are warned, "See to it that no one takes you captive through hollow and deceptive philosophy, which depends on human tradition and the basic principles of this world rather than on Christ" (Colossians 2:8).

Let's face it. There's a danger in disclosing the wiles of Satan. First, he doesn't like to have his cover pulled away. Like cockroaches who scurry under the cupboard when the light comes on, the dark prince wants to protect his aliases. Ritual killings by Satanists unmask evil, but to see Satan working in his innocent, charming disguises, we need our blinders removed.

We must be discerning on one hand, but avoid the other extreme of seeing Satan and his demons everywhere. Some people attribute thoughts and actions to demons that have no basis in biblical fact.

There is no such thing as the "lust demon" or the "anger demon" or the "demon of lies." We may lust or lie or lose our temper, and Satan may use these traits to lead us into disaster areas, but he cannot force us to act. The devil doesn't make us do it, we choose to initiate our own thoughts and actions.

Satan is working overtime for the minds of men today, and he will be increasingly active in a world-wide peace offensive. We can't count on dictators turning from terrorism to pacifism, even though the world desperately wants to believe these overtures of peace.

The man wearing a black hat, astride the white horse, will be accompanied by another rider who represents the very opposite of peace.

The Rider on the Red Horse

"Then another horse came out, a fiery red one. Its rider was given power to take peace from the earth and to make men slay each other. To him was given a large sword" (Revelation 6:4). When Jesus removes the second seal, the angel will summon the second horse. This blood-red beast is ridden by one who carries a "machaira," the assassin's sword which can cut the throat of an animal or a man.

The red horseman represents not only nation rising against nation and kingdom against kingdom, but man fighting against individual man. He ushers in a time of murder, assassination, bloodshed, and revolution. The massacre of students and civilians on June 4, 1989, in Beijing, China, which aroused the freedom-loving people of the world, is a microcosm of what will take place when the rider on the red horse brings his war machine into full force.

Are wars increasing in frequency and intensity? Twice in one generation, the world was plunged into world wars. Since World War II, the war that was to end all wars, there have been twelve limited wars, thirty-eight political assassinations, seventy-four rebellions for independence, 162 revolutions of either a political, economic, racial, or religious nature. As fast as we write these statistics, they are out of date.

When the second seal is opened, the message is the same as that of Jesus, "You will hear of wars and rumors of wars, but see to it that you are not alarmed. . . . For then there will be great distress, unequaled from the beginning of the world until now—and never equaled again. If those days had not been cut short, no one would survive . . " (Matthew 24:6, 21, 22).

How will those days be cut short? Who will survive this great holocaust? As our time table of things to come unfolds, we'll find the answers to these gnawing questions—questions that go unspoken in the minds of concerned men and women, for fear of creating personal depression or appearing to be negative thinkers.

The Black Horse of Famine

Have you ever been hungry?—I mean, really hungry, not just the need to satisfy your appetite, but the aching, clawing sensation that dominates every waking minute? I am the average American, taking the food in my cupboard for granted, seeing the waitress cart off leftovers, tossing out half-eaten apples. In America we have forgotten the old "waste not, want not" homily. We throw enough food in our garbage cans every day to feed a family of six for a day in India. Our dogs have a diet higher in protein than most of the people of the world.

When war comes, food is often in short supply. Some of you may remember the food stamps during World War II. The black horse of famine rides behind the red horse of war during the Tribulation, bringing world-wide starvation to the citizens of planet Earth.

As the third seal is broken, the scroll is unrolled to reveal the next event. John tells us ". . . there before me was a black horse! Its rider was holding a pair of scales in his hand. Then I heard what sounded like a voice among the four living creatures saying, 'A quart of wheat for a day's wages, and three quarts of barley for a day's wages, and do not damage the oil and the wine!'" (Revelation 6:6).

A quart of wheat is the least amount of food one person could eat to survive. The wage-earner will take his day's salary to the central government market and be measured out his ration. But what about the children and the elderly who cannot work? How will the worker be able to sustain his family?

Starving people scavenge for food and with the spirit of the Lord removed, they will kill to eat.

The rich and influential will have their "oil and wine," or the gourmet food from the deli. They will display their special pass, issued by the Great World Leader, and be able to stock their shelves with choice products from the state-owned supermarket, but the poor will starve.

The shadow of the coming of the black horse is hovering ominously over us at this time. Look at what's happening to the world's population. From the beginning of time until 1850, the world had one billion inhabitants; it took less than eighty years to pass the two billion mark in 1930 and only thirty-one years to reach three billion in 1961. Then the world's population really exploded: four billion in 1976 and five billion in 1989.

If we compare the world's resources to the gas tank on a car, we have passed the half-full point and are moving rapidly toward empty.

Ride a Pale Horse

"When the Lamb opened the fourth seal, I heard the voice of the fourth living creature say, 'Come!' I looked, and there before me was a pale horse. Its rider was named Death and Hades was following close behind him" (Revelation 6:7, 8).

John now sees two persons: Death is riding a pale horse and Hades is following close behind him. What power they have! They will kill a fourth of the earth by sword, famine, plague, and wild beasts. Armed with these weapons, the survival rate for the remaining population will be less and less.

God's "four sore judgments" are described as the "sword and famine, and the noisome beast, and the pestilence" (Ezekiel 14:21, KJV). History shows that there has been a close association between these four.

As a country is engulfed in war, the able-bodied men take up arms. Farmers leave their fields and food supplies become scarce. Soon there is malnutrition, followed by disease. Ultimately, the wild beasts prey upon the weakened people. Historians tell us that more people died of the epidemics of influenza and typhoid after World War I than died in the war itself.

Modern science seems to have eliminated the fear of plague, but today we may be on the verge of the worst plague the world has ever known. This deadly scourge could kill more people than have died in all of the pestilences yet known to man—it is the plague of AIDS.

Unlike the bubonic plague, which is caused by rats and other rodents, AIDS is transmitted by humans and tainted blood supplies. A person may be infected with the virus, but the deadly symptoms may not appear for years. The unsuspecting AIDS carrier may multiply this virus without knowing how many people are being infected.

Dr. William Hazeltine, a leading AIDS researcher at the Harvard Medical School, painted one of the most frightening pictures of AIDS yet put forth by any prominent scientist. He noted that perhaps a million people in the United States, and conceivably twenty million world-wide, had already been infected, even though only a small percentage had yet become sick.

"We must be prepared to anticipate that the vast majority of those now infected will ultimately, over a period of five to ten years, develop life-threatening illness," he said.[4]

Dr. James Curran of the Center for Disease Control wrote: ". . . in many areas, the number of persons infected with the AIDS virus is at least one hundred times greater than reported cases of AIDS."[5]

The pale horse of Death and Hades is not a welcome guest during this beginning of the seven years of Tribulation. Along with the plague will be the "beasts." I don't think this means that lions and tigers will be loosed throughout the earth, but it could be a symbolic meaning for beast-like men. The Greek word "beast" occurs thirty-eight times in the book of Revelation and in other places it refers to the Beast or the false Messiah.

I have another theory about these beasts, since they accompany famine and plague. The most destructive creature on the earth is the rat. He is a menace to human health and food supplies, and the nasty creature comes in more than 100 species. Rats are extremely prolific, producing five or more litters of eight to ten each year. It has been estimated that rats are responsible for the loss of more than one billion dollars worth of food each year in the United States alone. Their fleas carry bubonic plague, which destroyed one-third of the population of Europe in the fourteenth century.[6]

I recently heard of an animal rights advocate who allowed tree rats to come into his kitchen and ravage in the food, because he said, "They have a right to live, too."

For animal lovers everywhere, I would urge you to consider the fact that typhus killed an estimated 200 million people in four centuries, and the disease was transmitted by rat fleas.

And It's Only the Beginning

Jesus said, "All these are the beginning of sorrows" (Matthew 24:8, KJV). This is just the preface to the tribulation period. Before seven years have passed, the wrath of the Lord will be unleashed without restraint upon this earth.

Dear God, How Should I Feel?

Life is full of mixed emotions. I cannot look at those four horsemen without sensing the ambivalence in my heart. Knowing the Lord as my personal Savior, and believing what the Bible teaches about the Rapture, I am grateful that I won't be on earth to meet those evil riders. But every fiber of my soul mourns for those left on earth to suffer, while we who are believers will be in heaven with our Lord, worshiping the Lamb around the throne of God.

In Matthew 24, Jesus concludes His lesson on the future tribulation by telling a story about a fig tree. The parable reminds us that when the leaves come out on the tree, we know that summer is near. The lesson indicates that future events cast their shadows before them. When we see the problems of war, famine, death, and pestilence intensify, and other signs which are yet to be described, the time of Tribulation is getting closer.

Understanding prophecy should be the greatest motivation to telling others about Jesus Christ. Prophecy is the springboard for evangelism.

If I were a curiosity-seeker, a prophecy buff without a personal relationship with Jesus Christ, I'd hit the floor on both knees right now.

An ancient writer said it better than I could:

"How shall we escape if we ignore such a great salvation?" (Hebrews 2:3).

9

OF MARTYRS
AND MADNESS

Nothing the world has experienced to date will equal the grand-scale calamities of earth's final seven years. The first three and a half years of this period of time is called the Tribulation, the second half is the Great Tribulation.

The question that bothers many is, "How can a loving God cause these terrible events?" Part of the answer is found in the first book of the Bible, where we are told that Satan gained control of the earth in the Garden of Eden, through man's disobedience. Jesus Christ will regain that control forever. Meanwhile, all who oppose God must be judged before He returns to rule His kingdom.

Because of the amazing prediction by the Old Testament prophet, Daniel, 600 years before the birth of Jesus, we know the Tribulation will last seven years. Daniel was told by a messenger from God that there would be a period of "seventy 'sevens'" (490 years) in which God would use His chosen people, the Jews, to reach out to unbelievers. One specific event was to be the starting point of Jewish evangelistic activity, and that would be when the decree was given for the Jews to leave captivity in Babylon and return to rebuild Jerusulem. The 490-year prophetic time clock began in 445 B.C. when a Persian king, not realizing his part in God's great design for man, released the Jews from bondage to rebuild the walls (Nehemiah 2).

Daniel predicted that after 483 years the "Anointed One," meaning the Jewish Messiah, would be killed and within a time after that Jerusalem and the beautiful Temple would be destroyed. This prophecy was fulfilled to the day, because it was exactly 483 years after the decree to rebuild Jerusalem that Jesus proclaimed He was Israel's Messiah, was rejected and crucified. In A.D. 70, just as Daniel the prophet said, Titus and his Roman legions destroyed Jerusalem.

However, Daniel's prophecy of 490 years is seven years short. After Jesus was killed, God's special ambassadors became the church, comprised of both Jews and Gentiles. Since God never goes back on His promises, some day He will give the Jews a period of seven years to be His witnesses to the whole world.

What happened to the missing seven years? The book of Revelation solves the mystery Daniel presented. There is a time coming soon when the clock will start again for members of God's chosen people, a time when a team of 144,000 inspired Jewish evangelists will preach to the whole world. Earth has never experienced such crusades—imagine multiplying the outreach of Billy Graham, the man who has preached to more people than any other human, 144,000 times! Or imagine 144,000 apostle Pauls!

In the ninth chapter of Daniel, it is also prophesied that in the middle of the seven-year period, a diplomatic double-cross will take place when this powerful ruler will break his peace treaty with Israel and desecrate the sacred rebuilt Temple. If you go to Jerusalem today you will not see that Temple, but, as sure as I am writing this now, that place of Jewish worship will rise again.

The Scroll Continues to Unroll, the Seals Removed

The first four seals reveal the four horsemen and the beginning of judgments upon an unbelieving world. As the Antichrist enters the scene, conquering more and more of the earth's people, he is accompanied by wars and death and plagues. Many people will not fall for his flatteries and promises, and those rebels are eventually doomed. These are the martyrs whom John described: "I saw under the altar the souls of those who had been slain because of the word of God and the testimony they had maintained" (Revelation 6:9).

Haven't Jews been persecuted enough? As the Old Testament book of Exodus opened, the Pharaoh of Egypt planned to destroy all Jewish male children. Herod, in an attempt to kill the Christ child, ordered all the male children under the age of two in Bethlehem and vicinity to be murdered. Hitler was so filled with Satan that he sought to destroy all Jews on the European continent. The Antichrist will have the same evil intent during his reign.

The infamous Adolf Eichmann expressed his Nazi hatred for the Jews when he said, "I shall leap in my grave, for the thought that I have five million lives on my conscience is to me a source of inordinate satisfaction."[1]

The prediction of Moses concerning the Jews has literally been fulfilled throughout Jewish history:

"Then the Lord will scatter you among all nations, from one end of the earth to the other . . . among those nations you will find no repose, no resting place for the sole of your foot . . . You will live in constant suspense, filled with dread both night and day, never sure of your life" (Deuteronomy 28:64–66).

John tells us that the end of persecution is not over. During the Tribulation he sees the souls of those who will be slain. We can only imagine how they will be martyred and the suffering they will endure.

Remember, the church has been raptured and the dead in Christ have been resurrected, so these are not martyrs from the church age. When the church is gone, God is going to deal with Israel once more. Many Jews will turn to God in that day.

The question is asked, "How will people be saved in the Tribulation if all the believers are gone?" One way is through God's two witnesses who will be sent into the world prophesying and doing mighty deeds. We'll hear about these two miracle men later. Another way is through the 144,000 Jews "sealed" for God's service during this period. It is possible, however, that another means will be used. This would be through the "silent witness" that Dr. Henry Morris describes:

> Millions upon millions of copies of the Bible and Bible portions have been published in all major languages, and distributed throughout the world through the dedicated ministries of the Gideons, the Wycliffe Bible translators, and other such Christian organizations. Removal of believers from the world at the Rapture will not remove the Scriptures, and multitudes will no doubt be constrained to read the Bible in those days . . . Thus, many will turn to their Creator and Savior at that time, and will be willing to give their testimony for the Word of God and even to give their lives as they seek to persuade the world that the calamities they are suffering are judgments from the Lord."[2]

The next time you stay in a hotel or motel, pull open the top drawer of the dresser and look for the Gideon Bible. Imagine some distraught man, his wife and children mysteriously gone, picking up that Book soon after the great disappearing act. He doesn't know one Scripture from another, so he leafs through and sees the book of Acts.

I must act on something, he thinks. He reads what Peter said about Jesus. With each word, his heart is moved and soon his tears are falling on the thin pages. *It must be true, this is what my wife believed . . . but now she's gone.* "God save me!" he cries. "Salvation is found in no one else, for there is no other name under heaven given to men by which we must be saved" (Acts 4:12).

"Jesus, forgive me," he sobs, "save me from this hell on earth."

Don't forget that the regenerating ministry of the Spirit of God is not removed at the Rapture. His baptism into the body of Christ, His permanent indwelling ministry in each believer, and His restraining of sin will be finished. But when a sinner calls out for salvation, God will save him.

During the Tribulation, the new believers in Christ will be martyred in ways we cannot imagine. When the restraint of the Holy Spirit has been removed, the world rulers of that day will vent their hatred upon anyone who does not bow down to the Antichrist.

As the Tribulation believers read their contraband Bibles, they will begin to prophesy about more severe judgments to come. Preaching repentance and judgment will lead to their deaths at the hands of the new ruling regime.

Is this message heard in churches today? Judgment is not a popular concept, and yet Samuel, Isaiah, Jeremiah, Jonah, Paul, and Jesus preached judgment in their messages. Can we do any less?

Dr. W. A. Criswell reminds us of the true character of a prophet of God:

". . . whenever there is a true prophet of God, he will preach judgment. These modern so-called ministers of God speak all things nice. Modern pedagogical methods admonish never to mention things negative. Ignore them and they will not exist. There is not any hell and there is not any devil and there is not any judgment of God. All that is now intellectually passé. We have evolved beyond that . . . So we stand up and speak of the love of Jesus, and we speak of peace, and we speak of all things pretty and beautiful. But the same book that tells us about the good, tells us about the bad. The same revelation that speaks to us about heaven, speaks about hell."[3]

When the Surgeon General of the United States first issued dire warnings that smoking increased the possibilities of cancer, he wasn't very popular. But he saved lives.

I once read about a man who was so concerned from the newspaper articles about the dangers of smoking that he decided to give up the newspaper. Many today are like that with the Bible—just cancel it. . . .

When we talk about the judgment of God upon our sinful, unbelieving world, we may not be popular, but lives will be saved for eternity.

The Cry and Comfort of Martyrdom

"They called out in a loud voice, 'How long, Sovereign Lord, holy and true, until you judge the inhabitants of the earth and avenge our blood?' Then each of them was given a white robe, and they were told to wait a little longer, until the number of their fellow servants and brothers who were to be killed as they had been was completed" (Revelation 6:10, 11).

If these believing martyrs had been living in our time, their cry for vengeance would be wrong. In this present age, God is showing grace and mercy to the worst of men, and we are told to pray for them that despitefully use us. In the Tribulation, God will be meting out judgment; this cry of the new believers for revenge will be justified.

As I write this, I long for everyone to give their hearts to Christ now, when it is comparatively easy to be a Christian. During the Tribulation, the fate of believers will be worse than what happened in the Nazi prison camps during World War II.

Even during the worst of times, however, God's mercy is shown. When these martyrs ask how long it will be until they are avenged, they are told it will take a short period of time for the fulfillment of God's program, and that still other martyrs will be added to their number before final restitution.

Each martyr is rewarded with a robe. Scholars have been divided about the types of bodies these departed saints will have, for they will not receive their own resurrection bodies until the end of the Tribulation (Revelation 20:4, 5). But they must have something on which to hang a robe! Dr. John Walvoord interprets the passage this way:

> The martyred dead here pictured have not been raised from the dead and have not received their resurrection bodies. . . . A robe could not hang upon an immaterial soul or spirit. It is not the kind of body that Christians now have, that is the body of the earth, nor is it the resurrection body of flesh and bones of which Christ spoke after His own resurrection. It is a temporary body suited for their presence in heaven but replaced in turn by their everlasting resurrection body given at the time of Christ's return.[4]

Nothing can touch the believer unless it passes through the will of God. There is a definite plan for the life of every one of God's children; He has a purpose that explains each delay in His plan. These martyrs in the Tribulation are told to wait for judgment upon their enemies for a short time. Just as He numbers the hairs on our heads, He numbers the martyrs of the Tribulation period. There are two different times when the Jewish believers of the earth will be martyred: this particular time under the fifth seal, and a time later on in the Tribulation.

Today, there are many Jews who believe in Jesus as the Messiah. One man, a learned Russian Jew, was sent to Palestine over a quarter of a century ago to buy land for the Jews. While in Jerusalem, he went to the Mount of Olives to rest. He had been told to take a New Testament, as it was the best guidebook for the city.

The only Christ he had ever known was the Christ of the Greek and Roman churches, who were the persecutors of his people. As he read the New Testament, he became acquainted with the real Christ whom the Jewish Scriptures had foretold, and his heart grew warm. He looked off toward Calvary and thought: *Why are my people persecuted and cast out?* And his conviction gave the answer: *It is because we have put to death our Messiah.* He lifted his eyes to that Messiah and said, "My Lord and my God."

He came down from the Mount a disciple of the Lord Jesus Christ, and went home to Russia to erect a synagogue for the Jews, over the door of which was written: "Therefore let all the house of Israel know assuredly that God hath made that same Jesus, whom ye have crucified, both Lord and Christ" (Acts 2:36).

In the Tribulation, the testimony of that Russian Jew will be multiplied many times over.

Three and a Half Years Gone By

The sixth seal is to be broken (Revelation 6:12–16), and the earth is convulsed in a great upheaval of nature. One of the earthquakes to occur during the Tribulation rips across the world, devastating cities and countries and forcing men everywhere to cry out in terror.

Ask most Americans about earthquakes and they will talk about California. This is my home, and I have experienced some mild quakes; even those are enough to upset stomachs and equilibrium for hours. Earthquakes have been increasing in frequency and severity during the past one hundred years.

On October 17, 1989, San Francisco, Santa Cruz, and other Northern California cities were rocked by a terrifying quake that made it the third most lethal in U.S. history. The question which seemed uppermost in most Californians' minds was, "Is this the Big One?"

From the start, the scientists had the answer. They reported, "While it packed a punch, measuring 6.9 on the Richter scale, the 1906 quake was 25 times as strong, at 8:3. Warns Dallas Peck, director of the U.S. Geological Survey: 'The question is not whether a bigger earthquake is coming. The question is when.'"[5]

It's hard to imagine a scene more frightening than this cataclysmic earthquake midway in the Tribulation: the sun becoming black, the moon appearing as blood, the stars falling out of the sky, the mountains and islands of the sea being moved. But there is worse to come!

Matthew 24:15–21 teaches that marked increase in suffering comes right after the setting up of "the abomination of desolation" spoken of by Daniel, and this is to occur at midpoint in the Tribulation. The great world leader, the Antichrist, has been developing his plan to gain global control, and after three and half years of public adulation and oppression of the Jesus people, he will go to Jerusalem and march into the new Temple and proclaim that he is God (2 Thessalonians 2:4). This is the signal to believers on earth that the judgments unleashed will be worse than the ones before.

Prayers of the Damned

They will be sitting in their homes, reading the *Universal News,* or buying smog masks with their Global Credit Card, when the earth begins to shake. Before they can pull their hands out of the 666 sensor, the sky becomes black and a ghastly moon, covered with blood, appears upon the horizon. Against this eerie backdrop, the stars shoot to earth like a shower of white-hot coals. Mountains crumble into volcanic ash, islands sink into the sea, and clouds of dust spread across the sky, making it appear as if the sky were rolling.

Terrified, the earthdwellers race for any shelter they can find and pray to the mountains and rocks. "Hide us," they cry. "God is angry . . . help us escape from His wrath."

What a prayer meeting! The people will shout out to anything—even the mountains—for help. Their first instinct is to hide—get away from God. Isn't that what sin does to man? He covers up what he has done, thinking that he can escape the consequences. He turns his back on God's provision for sin and seeks help elsewhere.

As John describes this scene, I can imagine some man walking through the rubble left from the earthquake and crying out to his countrymen, "Listen to me. Repent—it's not too late to accept the Lord."

Creeping out from a cave, an ashen-faced man looks with hatred at the believer and snarls, "Get away from me, traitor—without the mark of the Beast it's you who are doomed to die."

In the midst of death, the hope of eternal life is offered, only to be refused by those with evil, nonrepentant hearts.

The avalanche of judgments will increase as the years of Tribulation advance, but instead of being convicted of their sins, the hearts of men and women will become harder.

10

REVIVAL DURING
HELL ON EARTH

Sherlock Holmes solved baffling crimes by deductive reasoning: "Elementary, my dear Watson." I always think of him with a magnifying glass, puffing on his pipe while examining clues. To many people, the prophecies of Revelation may seem like a mystery that needs an expert to unravel. However, just as good detectives review the facts in a case, we need to stop occasionally and examine what has been revealed so far in the mysterious events of the end times.

As the scroll continued to unroll, we have seen six seal judgments fall upon a groaning planet. The seeds of disaster spread with increasing intensity.

First, the white horse gallops onto the world scene carrying the man of deception, the coming world dictator; second, the red horse claws the air, abolishing any semblance of peace on earth; third, the black horse appears, creating hunger and economic disaster; fourth, the pale horse spreads deadly plague in its path. The fifth seal reveals the martyrs of the

Tribulation, and the sixth seal unleashes one of the most devastating earthquakes.

What a gloomy backdrop! No wonder the question is asked, ". . . who is able to stand?" (Revelation 6:17) Who can put up with these catastrophes without completely losing his mind? God knows the answer. He dispatches His special messengers in time of trouble.

First, He sends four angels to hold back the destruction to come on the earth, the sea, and the trees. Then a fifth angel commands, in a voice that reaches the four corners of the earth, that the next series of judgments shall not begin until servants of the living God have the seal on their foreheads. I believe this order may be given by Jesus Christ Himself.

What Is the Seal?

This is not the first time that God has sealed off some of His people from judgment. When He sent the flood upon the earth, He sealed Noah and his family from the rest of the human race; the flood didn't touch them. When He destroyed Jericho, He sealed Rahab and her household by means of a scarlet cord. Lot and his family escaped from Sodom before the fire fell. God sealed the first-born of all the Jewish families who were faithful by having them apply blood to the doorposts of their Egyptian homes.

It was a common custom in John's day for masters to seal or brand their slaves.

The seal of the Living God is not merely an external mark, but also a moral badge. God will choose 144,000 Jews for a very special earth-to-heaven mission.

In the day He calls and seals those Spirit-filled Jews, the power of their preaching will inspire others with tremendous courage. Have you ever known a genuine, devoutly converted Jew? He will put many Gentiles to shame in his bold witness for Christ. After all, only twelve Jews turned the first century upside down. Imagine what twelve thousand times twelve will do!

Who Receives the Stamp of Approval?

"Then I heard the number of those who were sealed: 144,000 from all the tribes of Israel" (Revelation 7:4).

This is one of the most important, and yet controversial, verses in the entire Bible. Many people want to be identified as part of the 144,000, but only the Jews qualify to be chosen.

Remember, the church is already in heaven; all true believers have been raptured before this time. Some people have substituted the church for Israel, which is gross error and confuses the unity of the Bible. J. A. Seiss wrote:

"As I read the Bible, when God says 'children of Israel,' I do not understand Him to mean any but people of Jewish blood, be they Christians or not; and when He speaks of the twelve tribes of the sons of Jacob, and gives the names of the tribes, it is impossible for me to believe that He means the Gentiles, in any sense or degree, whether they be believers or not."[1]

The sealed ones are not the Seventh-Day Adventists. These folks believe that the 144,000 are members of their church who are found observing the Jewish Sabbath when the Lord comes back again, and they are raptured up to glory. For this to be true, every Seventh-Day Adventist would have to be Jewish in lineage and from one of the twelve tribes.

They are not the cult known as Jehovah's Witnesses. This group used to claim that all of their members were in this number, but when they grew to more than 144,000 members, they had to revise their teaching.

But Why the Jews?

But God chose the Jews; they have a very special place in God's plan.

Look at the way the Jews have been used. With a few exceptions, the majority of the authors who were chosen to write the Bible were Jewish. They not only wrote God's Word, they preserved it. During the lifetime of many of us, the discovery of the Dead Sea Scrolls is a vivid example of how Jewish scribes copied and cherished those parchments. The date of Isaiah's scroll is 200 B.C., and it proved to be almost identical to an Isaiah manuscript dated A.D. 900. Imagine how many generations of father to son, tribe to tribe, those words must have traveled.

Our Savior was a Jew—however, the majority of Jews have not accepted Him. Even though many Jewish believers have a zealousness for the Lord that shames Gentiles, as a nation and a group they have been blinded to Him. This will end some day. Romans 11:25 says, "I do not want you to be ignorant of this mystery, brothers, so that you may not be conceited: Israel has experienced a hardening in part until the full number of the Gentiles has come in. And so all Israel will be saved. . . ."

The full number of Gentiles will come in at that moment of time when the church is removed by the Rapture. Then God's special focus and blessing will shift back to Israel. Spirit-filled Jewish evangelists will evangelize the whole world in seven years, a task their nation has not been able to accomplish in the past 2,000 years.

Protective Custody

Why are the 144,000 sealed? As we see the judgments of the tribulation period becoming more and more severe, the hatred of the Antichrist and his followers increasing, doesn't it make sense that God would protect His own until their work is finished? Just as the three Hebrew children were kept alive in the fire, so these sealed Jews will be protected throughout the last seven years before the return of Christ. God will send them for a powerful task: these Jews will preach the gospel in such a way that multitudes will believe.

They are sealed because of God's promise; they will enter the kingdom at the end of the Tribulation to reign with Christ and His glorified church. They are kept from harm during the Tribulation so that they might be alive when the Millennium begins, thus fulfilling God's covenant promises to His people.

Not all of the believers will be given the same protective custody. The seal for believers will be very visible on their foreheads. Whatever that seal may be, we can be certain it will be starkly different from the mark of the Antichrist. There will be no "closet" Christians in that day.

I have watched Billy Graham crusades and have been overwhelmed by the hundreds and thousands of people who respond to a simple, straightforward gospel message. Can you imagine how it will be when those Jewish Billy Grahams begin to preach? Stadiums will not be able to hold the masses. As they leave the sites of these evangelistic rallies, the gestapo of the Antichrist will probably be waiting at the gates, searching for those who have the seal of God.

Safety for New Saints

Several times during Revelation, God allows us to see ahead to better days. It's a relief to know that the light at the end of the tunnel is still burning brightly. Without it, we might become utterly depressed.

In one prophetic leap into the future, we glimpse a revival that will have believers dancing in the aisles. Heaven will resound with the sound of music.

When the Tribulation is over, the people who have been won to Christ by the 144,000 evangelists will be out of their earthly misery and into a glorious new world. John saw a great multitude of people from every nation and language, standing before the throne of God, in front of Jesus. These new believers will be dressed in white robes and carrying palm branches— surrounding them will be angels and the twenty-four elders. A great celebration will take place in heaven.

As this enthusiastic choir is singing, the angels, elders, and four living creatures fall down and worship God. Can you imagine how they will feel, seeing all these sinners enter the kingdom? We hear how the angels rejoice over one sinner who is saved, imagine what they will do when all these saints come marchin' in!

When we begin to see the incredible disasters the world will experience during the Tribulation, we can understand how these people will be praising the Lord with such fervor. Their troubles will be over. They will be home at last.

"Therefore, they are before the throne of God and serve him day and night in his temple; and he who sits on the throne will spread his tent over them. Never again will they hunger; never again will they thirst. The sun will not beat upon them, nor any scorching heat" (Revelation 7:15, 16).

This is in stark contrast to what happened to them on earth. They had been hungry, for they couldn't buy food without the mark of the beast; they were thirsty, for the rivers were turned to blood; they were scorched by the burning sun. But now, the agony of their lives will be over.

Prophecy students have frequently said that the whole world needs to hear the gospel before Christ returns. This is true, but it is not a condition that needs to be met before the Rapture. This hearing must occur before the second coming of Christ. If the whole world needed to hear the gospel before the Rapture, there would be no reason for the 144,000 evangelists during the Tribulation, and there would be no Tribulation saints. Isn't that an interesting thought?

Why Bother Being Saved Now?

Many people have said words like this to me: "Life is too short. I'll have my fling while I'm still around. When the Tribulation starts, if it's really true, I'll be saved by the first Jewish evangelist I hear."

What a frightening idea! In the first place, as we continue with John in his travels into the future, we would not want to be on earth during those devastating seven years. Also, many who are living during the Tribulation will not be saved because they will fall under the spell of Satan's lies. The Bible says:

"The coming of the lawless one will be in accordance with the work of Satan displayed in all kinds of counterfeit miracles, signs and wonders, and in every sort of evil that deceives those who are perishing. They perish because they refused to love the truth and so be saved" (2 Thessalonians 2:9, 10).

In this present age, Satan's lies keep people from believing the truth. In the Tribulation age, it will be the same.

There is no second chance for those who have heard the gospel and refused it. The Bible teaches that those who have heard the gospel before the Rapture and rejected Jesus Christ, will not have another opportunity to be saved after Christ comes for His own.

Sticks and Stones

As we approach the Third Millennium, and Christ has not returned, those of us who speak and write about the end of the world as we know it will continue to be labeled the "gloom and doom" people. A friend sent me a newspaper article, written by a columnist who warned that we should get ready for what he called "millennia mania." The writer cited that not only theologians, but also novelists and economists were cashing in on the fears of Armageddon.

I'm not concerned about being a target for such accusations. The Bible told of these events long before I was born. With all the prophecies of the past being fulfilled in the life and times of Jesus, with world events accelerating in prophetic fulfillment, I can only ask, "How long will it take for people to see the truth?"

End of Parenthesis

Chapter seven of Revelation is a parenthesis before the seventh seal is opened. It is a flashback to the start of evangelistic activity and provides a panorama of salvation during the Tribulation. We have seen how God provides an opportunity for His ancient people, the Jews, to be obedient to Him in a way they have never been.

What an encouragement! Even during the Tribulation, God understands the needs of the human heart and gives both Jews and Gentiles who have not heard the Gospel before an opportunity to enter the kingdom.

God Reveals the Future . . . But Not Our Future

Salvation is forever, but a decision is for the moment. When Charles Colson was told about "accepting Christ," he was cynical at first. He said to his Christian friend, "I saw men turn to God in the Marine Corps; I did once myself. Then afterwards it's all forgotten and everything is back to normal. Foxhole religion is just a way of using God."[2]

With his world crashing about him, Colson read a book, *Mere Christianity,* by C. S. Lewis, and his pride and "protective armor," as he called it, began to be penetrated by God's truth. He realized that the central thesis of Lewis's book was: *Jesus Christ is God.*

He wrote in his book, *Born Again,* "While I sat alone staring at the sea I love, words I had not been certain I could understand or say fell naturally from my lips: 'Lord Jesus, I believe You. I accept You. Please come into my life. I commit it to You.'"[3]

Colson did not know what his future would be, nor how God would lead him to minister to millions with the testimony of his life. We do not know what our future holds, either. A swerving car, a pain in the chest, a brick falling from a building, an earthquake or tornado, could end one's earthly life today. However, we can know for certain where we're going to spend our eternal future. He solves that mystery for us with clues that are written in **bold type**. No magnifying glass is needed.

11

SILENCE BEFORE
THE STORM

When the trees stand lifeless and the atmosphere is heavy with humidity, tension builds in the air. The old dog, usually sprawled on the grass in the front yard, stands with his ears quivering. Overhead, the sky is gray, foreboding. Suddenly, the spell is broken as lightning streaks across the sky and thunder shakes the windowpanes.

Before the next series of plagues is described, there is a dramatic pause. The conductor's baton is raised and the orchestra is waiting for his signal to begin the overture. The last or seventh seal is not unrolled by the Lion of the tribe of Judah until ". . . there was silence in heaven for about half an hour" (Revelation 8:1).

How can our limited minds describe silence in heaven? It's like catching your breath before making a ten-meter dive into a cold swimming pool, or preparing to walk on stage before a thousand people.

Silence. Perhaps God wanted to give His beloved friend, John, a chance to prepare for the awesome events to come. John sees seven angels standing before God and holding seven sound-less trumpets. In the Old Testament, the trumpet announced important events and gave signals in times of war—listen, earth, they are saying, something mighty is about to happen; citizens' alert, judgment is coming.

The first trumpet sounds: hail and fire, mixed with blood, pour out of the sky, burning a third of the trees and a third of all the green grass. Blackened land, charred and smoldering, covers America, Europe, Australia, Africa, and all the continents. Wildlife dies. Death emits its acrid odors. I believe the earth will experience an ecological upheaval that will make our toxic dumps seem like playgrounds.

The second trumpet hurls "something like a huge mountain" (Revelation 8:8) into the sea and turns a third of the sea to blood, killing a third of all life in the seas and oceans and destroying a third of the ships.

Imagine the chaos on the cruise ships and the cargo carriers after this catastrophic event. The naval fleets of every major country will be crippled beyond help. Seafood will be rationed, restaurants will go out of business, and the source of heart-healthy food will dwindle.

When the third angel sounds his trumpet, a torch-like star falls from the sky, turning a third of the water into bitter-tasting liquid which poisons all who drink it. The name of the star is "Wormwood," which is a plant right out of the killing fields. (And do you remember the bumbling devil by that name in C. S. Lewis's *Screwtape Letters*?)

Today we are faced with increased pollution of our drinking water, but in that future day the fresh water supply will become as putrid as a Calcutta gutter.

When the fourth angel sounds his trumpet, the earth will become darkened. The sun, moon, and stars will lose a third of their light. This fits Luke's prophecy: "There will be signs in the sun, moon and stars. On the earth, nations will be in anguish and perplexity at the roaring and tossing of the sea. Men will faint from terror, apprehensive of what is coming on the world, for the heavenly bodies will be shaken" (Luke 21: 25, 26).

Ecological Nightmare

God is able to cause any of the miracles in the book of Revelation, without our analogies to current events. However, John had to give his first-century interpretation to the incredible view into the future. In our nuclear age, these ecological disasters become increasingly possible.

In just one short generation, pollution has become the pall over our cities, spreading through ground water contamination into the countryside. Man has progressed scientifically, medically, and technologically, but he is destroying God's earth in the process. Our grandparents and great-grandparents would have laughed at the thought of purchasing water-treatment systems for their homes, or air-treatment systems for their offices and bedrooms.

Even without God's intervention, the earth is being handed over to the greatest polluter of all time, Satan himself.

Planet Earth is in a state of preparation for someone to solve its problems.

Woe! Woe! Woe!

I've never heard an eagle speak, but John did, and the message was not a cheerful one. At the end of Revelation chapter eight an eagle calls out loudly, "Woe! Woe! Woe to the inhabitants of the earth, because of the trumpet blasts about to be sounded by the other three angels!" (8:13).

The Antichrist may be sitting in his war room, planning global military strategy. Soon his troops will be reinforced by an army of demons.

Oozing from the Abyss

As the fifth angel sounds his trumpet, a divine agent in the form of an angel falls out of the sky and enters earth's hemisphere. This angel has a key to open a subterranean abode described as "the Abyss" (Revelation 9:1, 2).

Smoke billows from this prison house of evil, unleashing the soot of hell. A spiritual plague of demonic proportions breaks out upon the whole earth, fueled by the work of millions of demon creatures.

This unnamed personality who has fallen from heaven is none other than Satan. It is the second time he has been kicked out of heaven. The first time he was ousted predates the creation of man and is described by Jesus: "I saw Satan fall like lightning from heaven" (Luke 10:18); and also by the prophet Isaiah: "How art thou fallen from heaven, O Lucifer, son of the morning! how art thou cut down to the ground, which didst weaken the nations!" (Isaiah 14:12, KJV).

Satan and his demonic cohorts are not released without God's permission. When the bottomless pit is opened, all the creatures who have been incarcerated from the beginning swarm out. They have the appearance of locusts and swarm over the earth to torture the masses of people who do not have the seal of God upon their foreheads.

These spirits from the lower world will bear the likeness of several animals: horses, lions, and scorpions. Some will look like men. They will be hideous, but powerful, invincible, indestructible, and intelligent. What would a swarm of demons be like when released from a hell where they have been chained for thousands of years? It would be impossible to understand this whole scene apart from the vivid descriptions in Revelation 9:1–12.

The venerable Bible scholar, Harry Ironside, said: "It is quite difficult to express the effect produced by the sight of the whole atmosphere filled on all sides and to a great height by an innumerable quantity of these insects, whose flight was slow and uniform and whose noise that of rain."[1]

The "pit" that has been the home of the demons is the Greek word for "abyss." We have a picture of a vast depth approached by a shaft, whose top is covered. It is a sobering thought to realize that many of the demons of hell are not free to hurt us in this present age. Satan is managing to do a good job of destruction today without his entire war corps to back him up.

Damage of Demons from the Pit

Hitler was demon-possessed: He changed a generation and temporarily altered the course of history. What will be the result of countless thousands of demons running unchecked throughout the earth during this time of the Tribulation? It will be a Dachau/Buchenwald type of experience for those who are left to endure it.

It will be painful. "They had tails and stings like scorpions, and in their tails they had power to torment people for five months" (Revelation 9:10). The sting of scorpions is not lethal, but as the poison enters the system it literally sets the nerve center on fire.

This torment is so painful that the agony will last for five months. Yes, the Bible is that exact. There are some people, however, who will escape this torture. The people with the seal of God on their foreheads will be exempt.

"During those days men will seek death, but will not find it; they will long to die, but death will elude them" (Revelation 9:6). Imagine the agony when some attempt suicide, but find it impossible. The gun doesn't fire, the poison is ineffective, the leap from a tall building is interrupted by a net! Strange days, indeed.

Walter Scott summarized the strategy of these demon creatures:

> These scorpion locusts overrun the once Holy Land, and prey upon the unsealed and ungodly part of Israel. The venom of falsehood, born in the pit—doctrines, teachings and principles conceived in the abyss are received by the apostate part of the nation, and create in their souls and consciences intolerable anguish. Without God, given up judicially by Him to receive Satan's lies and delusions, little wonder that they, his dupes and disciples, share so far as men on earth can, the full misery.

The scorpion-like tales of the locusts contain the moral poison which so awfully torments those who receive it. There lies the venomous stings, and the power to torment.[2]

Good Angels and Bad Angels

The Sunday school program with our children sprouting wings is not a completely accurate depiction of angels. There are two kinds of angels in the Bible. On the one hand, we were introduced to good angels who held back the four winds of the earth, restraining the forces of evil in Revelation chapter seven. On the other hand, during the last half of the Great Tribulation, four evil angels will be released who have been bound at the Euphrates River. The Bible tells us that the exact hour, day, month, and year have been set when these sinister characters are loosed at the sounding of the sixth trumpet (Revelation 9:13–14). The orders for this deadly quartet are devastating, for they will kill a third of mankind remaining on earth.

Who is left? The pale horse of Revelation 6:8 has already killed one-fourth of the world's population. Now, one-third of the remaining inhabitants are killed. This leaves only one-half of the original number alive on the earth. Never since Noah has such a substantial proportion of the earth's population come under God's righteous judgment.

March across the River Bed

Swarming over the land in this judgment is an army of 200 million mounted troops. Some think this is an army of demons, but I believe there is another possible identity of this massive army, and Revelation 16:12 gives us a clue: "The sixth angel poured out his bowl on the great river Euphrates, and its water was dried up to prepare the way for the kings from the East." This could denote China and her allies, which today is very plausible. When John wrote this prophecy there were not even 200 million people on earth. It is estimated that by the year 2000 the Chinese population would be at least 1.35 billion. It is not difficult to imagine that there could be a soldier for every 7,000 civilians. This number is almost twice as many troops as the Allied and Axis powers combined, when they were at peak strengths in World War II.

For centuries, the idea of drying up the mighty Euphrates seemed ridiculous. Today, man is accomplishing what God could do with a flick of His divine finger. The foreshadow of this miracle was performed, "With the push of a button at the new Ataturk Dam last week, Turkey's President Turgut Ozal cut the flow of the Euphrates River to Syria and Iraq, his country's arid downstream neighbors, by 75 percent."[3]

During the Tribulation, vast numbers of soldiers will march across the dry Euphrates river bed in a procession one mile wide and eighty-seven miles long. Their role in the Battle of Armageddon is crucial. As they descend upon the scene for the last great battle of the world, a full-scale military war will wipe out a third of mankind. It's no secret that China possesses a nuclear arsenal today and could unleash it, just as they mowed down the students in Tiananmen Square. Their slogan, inscribed on the Gate of Heavenly Peace, says "Long Live the Unity of the Peoples of the World!" Some day that noble desire will be a mockery.

It is possible that during the false peace brought about in the early phases of that time between the Rapture and the Second Coming, there will be disarmament of some kind. After a few short years, however, modern means of war will be fully used once again.

Granite Hearts

"The rest of mankind that were not killed by these plagues still did not repent" (Revelation 9:20).

This is one of the most astounding verses in Revelation. Wouldn't you think that by this time the remaining earth survivors would fall down before God and beg for mercy? But no—their flinty eyes will be hard, their mouths pursed in mockery. Nuclear war, earthquakes, plagues, deadly insects, people dying faster than babies being born, these disasters won't break the pagans. They will continue to worship materialism and make idols of their possessions.

They will be religious, of course. The very fiber of man's being longs for some belief, for religious experience. They will worship demons and idols that are made of gold, silver, bronze, stone, and wood. We're seeing this adulation today in the fashion industry, touting everything from crystal amulets to skull bracelets. One owner of a jewelry boutique said that the macabre side of religion is big business.

Satan and his CEO, Antichrist, will be working to get people to worship him as he has always wanted to be worshiped. Wholeheartedly.

During this phase of the Tribulation, four sins will be rampant: murder, sorceries, sexual immorality, and thefts. The lifestyles of the rich and infamous will be completely depraved.

Our inner cities in America are fraught with gang wars. Murder and random shootings are reported daily, but during the Tribulation, murder will be so common that it probably won't be reported. Where the gospel is unknown, human life is cheap.

Over a century ago, before we groaned under the present crime wave, J. A. Seiss, author of *The Apocalyse,* predicted, on the basis of Revelation 9:21, that capital punishment would be largely abolished by the time of the Tribulation.

The second prominent sin will be drug use and occult practices. When I was a child, drugs meant aspirin or some cherry-flavored cough medicine the doctor prescribed. The occult meant poking pins into voodoo dolls. How far we've progressed (or regressed) to this present time! Drug use, witchcraft, and sorcery will rage in the last part of the Tribulation. I used to wonder how people could be so immune to the disasters surrounding them, until I realized they would be using so many mind-altering drugs that reality and fantasy would be intertwined.

Dr. Henry Morris points to the relationship between drugs and the occult:

"Stupefying and hallucinatory drugs have been associated with sorcery and witchcraft for ages, yielding to their users strange visions and hallucinations, which they could interpret as oracles for the guidance of their clients. Also, they divested their users of the control of their own minds, making them easily available for possession and control by evil spirits."[4]

The third great sin of the Tribulation period is rampant immorality—all types of sexual activity outside of the bounds of married love. When the world no longer fears God, there will be nothing to check the wildest indulgence of lust. The family unit will be almost unknown, men and women will simply indulge themselves like animals.

The fourth big sin will be "thefts." With all laws relaxed and with mutual respect almost gone, greed will be the great motivator as those who survive try to prey off each other. This will no doubt include burglaries and armed robberies, as well as embezzlement and fraud.

Are we seeing a prelude to the four big sins prevalent during the Tribulation? Look at the mess that exists in America today! *Time* magazine in 1987 had a cover story that boldly asked, "What Ever Happened to Ethics?" The byline read, "Assaulted by sleaze, scandals, and hypocrisy, America searches for its moral bearings." Can we ever return to a nation of unlocked doors—or business agreements sealed with a handshake? Will our urban streets be safe again? Will "living-together arrangements" be only after the wedding ceremony? You answer. I'm afraid I can't.

Storm Warnings

Did you know there are over 600 warnings in the Bible about judgment and evil? The judgments that will take place on earth are just a small glimpse of an eternal hell. It is a place of fire and smoke. It is a place of pain, as pictured by the stinging scorpions. Hell is a place of crying. Hell is a place where a person cannot die. How could anyone survive in a place of such agony? Here is one answer: the natural bodies we now have could not survive! However, those who have denied Christ, just as those who have accepted Him, will receive new bodies. They will not be glorified bodies in the image of Jesus Christ, but composed in such a manner that they will be able to endure the fiery torments without being destroyed. The rich man in Luke 16 did not perish in the torment of hell. Instead, he called out to have Lazarus, a beggar in heaven, take pity on him and give him some water to cool his tongue, "because I am in agony in this fire."

Hell is not a place where good ol' boys sit around and drink beer and play poker to pass the time.

But our Lord is compassionate. He does not want anyone to receive the gruesome sentence of eternal hell. He begs: "'As surely as I live, declares the Sovereign Lord, I take no pleasure in the death of the wicked, but rather that they turn from their ways and live. Turn! Turn from your evil ways! Why will you die, O house of Israel?'" (Ezekiel 33:11).

Likewise, I find no pleasure in describing about the times of terror the unsaved will experience. As Vance Havner said, "The real test of how much we believe of prophetic truth is what we are doing to warn men to flee from the wrath to come . . . to believe the solemn truths of prophecy and then make our way complacently through a world of sin and shame is not merely unfortunate, it is criminal."[5]

12

GOD IS STILL IN CHARGE

Where were you, God, when the baby died? Where were you when the missionaries were massacred? Why do bad guys seem to win and good guys lose? The time is coming when God is going to deal with those questions once and for all. Revelation 10:7 says: ". . . the mystery of God will be accomplished, just as he announced to his servants the prophets." We will see the puzzle of the ages solved.

What Has Happened So Far?

We have been following the removal of the seals from the seven-sealed book which was taken from God by Christ, the lion of the tribe of Judah. As each seal is removed, judgment is dealt to the world. In the last seal, judgments are intensified through the blowing of seven trumpets by seven angels. These trumpet judgments will be more devastating and ruthless than the six seals before them. When the seventh trumpet sounds, we will see how the bowl judgments will be so terrible that they bring the world, as we know it, to an end!

We have an interlude described by John before the seventh trumpet sounds its dreadful notes. I, for one, am relieved. God gives us hope, just when we may be wondering if He is losing this war and evil is winning.

The Divine Interludes

An interlude is like a parenthesis. When a parenthesis is used in writing, it usually contains information that is necessary for the reader to have. There are several of these interludes in this prophetic picture: the first between the judgments of the sixth and seventh seal judgments (the silence in heaven). Now, between the sounding of the sixth and seventh trumpet we find the longest interlude of all.

In the midst of God's wrath, we see His mercy. However depressing the events might seem, God is not without His witness, and from some special messengers we will find out what words of encouragement He has.

I can empathize with the depression John must have felt. Through his eyes we have seen some upcoming events so heavy that by now we may be thinking, *How can I stand to hear more?*

On the day I was writing this chapter there was a sharp earthquake in Northern California (this was not the "big little one" of October 1989). A young man, awakened from a sound sleep, panicked and plunged to his death from a fifth-story apartment window. Apparently the shock drove him to irrational behavior. He was literally scared to death.

God does not allow us to be "scared to death" in His unveiling of things to come, but to be shaken to life. In the tenth chapter of Revelation He gives John a future glimpse of His triumph over the earth, even though the ultimate victory of Christ will not come until after the pouring out of the seventh vial.

The Messenger from Heaven

"Then I saw another mighty angel coming down from heaven. . . ."

We have met this angel twice before in the book of Revelation. Once he held back impending judgments in order that the 144,000 could be sealed. Another time he arrived to pour out fire and judgment upon the earth. Now he comes as King, taking back possession of the earth.

Angels appear over sixty times in Revelation, not counting the seven angels of the churches. Although the identity of this messenger from heaven seems clear to me, there has been quite a controversy about who he is. I believe this angel is the Angel of Jehovah, the Lord Himself.

This heavenly messenger will be clothed with a cloud, just as deity is often described. Science has its explanation for clouds, but I like to think that God made them for His special clothing.

The messenger will be crowned with a rainbow. The rainbow has always been associated with God's promise to Noah not to destroy the earth again by water (Genesis 9:13). Now we have an assuring promise from God that there is mercy in His judgment.

The poet, Wordsworth, wrote "My heart leaps up when I behold a rainbow in the sky." John must have felt the same way when he saw this important messenger. Revelation takes us on a roller-coaster of emotions, from heartache and depression to joyous celebration.

He takes possession of heaven and earth, standing triumphantly astride the land and the sea. When he makes an announcement, it's so loud that Satan's roar seems like a whisper.

". . . his face was like the sun, and his legs were like fiery pillars. He was holding a little scroll, which lay open in his hand. He placed his right foot on the sea and his left foot on the land, and he gave a loud shout like the roar of a lion" (Revelation 10:2).

"When he shouted, the voices of the seven thunders spoke. And when the seven thunders spoke, I was about to write, but I heard a voice from heaven say, 'Seal up what the seven thunders have said and do not write it down'" (Revelation 10:3, 4).

This is like a seven-gun salute in the skies—it sounds like something Hollywood would orchestrate. Job said, "God's voice thunders in marvelous ways; he does great things beyond our understanding" (37:5).

What did He tell John in the seven thunders? We don't know. In the midst of His detailed instructions, He issues a strange order. The first and only time in this book, John is forbidden to reveal the content of the message of the seven thunders. It seems to me that since God said they were sealed up, we ought to leave them sealed. We will have an opportunity to satisfy our curiosity about the "secret things" of the Lord during eternity.

This Is It!

The mighty angel shouted, "There will be no more delay!" (Revelation 10:6). This is the announcement that time has run out. The race is over, the curtain has come down, the Lord's return is at hand. (We still have more characters and events of the end times to introduce; but remember, the Lord is giving John a glimpse into the future.)

Throughout time there has been frustration of why God is delaying. The souls under the altar asked about God's time schedule. The disciples came to Jesus privately and asked, ". . . Tell us . . . what will be the sign of your coming and of the end of the age?" (Matthew 24:3).

Scoffers have taunted and saints have pleaded, and no one, not even the angels of heaven, know when the Lord will return. Now He tells John, "But in the days when the seventh angel is about to sound his trumpet, the mystery of God will be accomplished, just as he announced to his servants the prophets" (Revelation 10:7).

What mystery is this? I believe the mystery that will be revealed at the end of the Tribulation is the mystery of the silence in heaven. It has appeared that sin has run unchecked and evil has been unbridled. But here, in this end time, at this last moment, the mystery will be finished. Walter Scott said:

> Does it not seem strange that Satan has been allowed for 6000 years to wrap and twist his coils around the world, to work evil and spoil and mar the work of God? . . . Is it not a mystery why God, the God of righteousness and holiness, allows evil to go unpunished and His own people to be crushed and broken on every hand? Truly this is the mystery of God. . . . God bears with evil till the hour of judgment arrives, when he will avenge the cry of His elect, and come out of His place to punish the wicked . . . evil, now tolerated and allowed, will be openly punished. The mystery is at an end. Christ is about to reign.[1]

A Bittersweet Order

John has been a spectator watching the unfolding events, just as we have. Now he becomes an actor in the drama of the Apocalypse. He hears a voice from heaven, telling him to take the little book which the mighty angel is holding and eat it. This seems to be a strange order, until we realize that tasting and eating in the Bible often refers to hearing or believing, just as the prophet Ezekiel was told to eat a scroll containing bitter words. (Maybe this is where the expression, "eat your words," came from.)

The book that John is asked to eat lists all the judgments that would be poured out upon the world. It was a command to digest the truth of prophecy and be ready to go to the nations with a warning. He was to saturate himself with God's Word so that it was literally a part of him. This is the kind of spiritual involvement that all preachers should have before they open their mouths to declare God's truth.

John was warned that the book would be sweet to the

taste, but bitter in his belly. I can relate to this! As I study prophecy I get so excited, knowing that the Lord has a new world waiting for us. Other times I become downright depressed when I think of the fate of those who hear, but reject the truth. The same gospel that makes it possible for me to go to heaven, puts someone else in hell.

Preaching prophetic truth is a bitter-sweet experience.

Puzzle of the Rebuilt Temple

In Revelation 11, John, as the actor in this prophetic odyssey, is told by the Divine Director to act out the prophecy of the rebuilt temple that the regathered Jews will build in Jerusalem. "I was given a reed like a measuring rod and was told, 'Go and measure the temple of God and the altar, and count the worshipers there'" (11:1).

The Old Testament prophet Ezekiel said the Jews will go back to Jerusalem in unbelief: "For I will take you out of the nations; I will gather you from all the countries and bring you back into your own land . . ." (36:24). The Jews will build a temple in the name of Jehovah God, but they will not know Him at all.

Go to Jerusalem today and you will look in vain for the temple. Standing on the temple mount is the Dome of the Rock, the third holiest Moslem shrine. Its brilliant Persian tiles and soaring golden dome dominate one of the most fiercely contested pieces of real estate in the world. For nearly 2,000 years, Jews, Moslems, and Christians have been slaughtered in their attempts to control this plot of land.

In the first millennium B.C., Solomon's magnificent temple dominated Jerusalem. Destroyed by Nebuchadnezzar, Babylon's reigning king, in 587 B.C., it was lavishly rebuilt by King Herod. Many of the events of Jesus' life centered around this temple. However, He prophesied that not one stone of those great buildings would be left standing, and in A.D. 70, Titus laid siege to Jerusalem, massacring the populace and destroying Herod's temple. The only remnant of the second temple is the Western Wall, where Jews come to pour out their anguish and grief, and plead for their Messiah to come.

Daniel prophesied that a covenant would be signed between the Antichrist and the leader of the Jewish people and that after three and a half years the Antichrist would break the treaty and desecrate the temple. This clash would usher in the last three and a half years of the Great Tribulation. The Temple must be rebuilt for this to occur.

Until the Six-day War in June 1967, the Jews would not have been able to rebuild the Temple, for they did not have sovereign rule of the Old City. When the cease-fire was called in what the *Encyclopedia Americana* called "one of the most decisive campaigns in the annals of war," the jubilant Israelis once more had possession of the Old City.

In a scholarly book on the *Dome of the Rock,* the writer said, "Six hundred and fifty-seven years to the day on which the Babylonians had plundered and razed the first Temple, its successor fell. The Jewish Temple would never rise again."[2] He was wrong, for the Bible clearly indicates that the temple must be present for the Antichrist to desecrate it as Antiochus Epiphanes did in 168 B.C.

The Antichrist will set himself up as God in that temple: "Don't let anyone deceive you in any way, for that day will not come until the rebellion occurs and the man of lawlessness is revealed, the man doomed to destruction. He will oppose and will exalt himself over everything that is called God or worshiped, so that he sets himself up in God's temple, proclaiming himself to be God" (2 Thessalonians 2:3, 4).

For many years, scholars have thought that the temple would be rebuilt on the exact location of the present Mosque of Omar. This would mean the destruction of the Moslem shrine before any temple building could be accomplished. Do you think the Moslems would stand by and allow this to happen? They would marshal every gun-carrying defender they have for such a holy outrage.

That clash may never happen. Some important archaeo-
logical discoveries by Dr. Asher Kaufman, professor of physics
at Hebrew University, were revealed in the *Biblical Archeology
Review,* indicating that the actual location of Solomon's and
Herod's temples was twenty-six meters away from the Dome of
the Rock. If this study is valid, the third temple could be built
without disturbing the Dome of the Rock![3]

Whatever scholars say or doubters write, the temple will
be rebuilt.

When John is asked to measure the temple, he is sup-
plied with a measuring rod. Whenever the word "rod" is used
in Revelation, it refers to judgment. What is John measuring?
I believe it is a symbol of the Lord's own people, the Jews.
They are still in unbelief at the time of the measuring, and
some will never change throughout the Tribulation.

All is not lost. In the midst of devastating circumstances,
God has His witnesses. Two men will walk unharmed upon
the earth during the first half of the Tribulation. Although they
are introduced in Revelation 11, they begin their work of witnessing to the world after the Rapture.

Just as we will see that Satan has his two men—the Beast
and the false prophet—so God has His two men. And what a
pair they are!

I.D. for Two Witnesses

"And I will give power to my two witnesses, and they will
prophesy for 1,260 days, clothed in sackcloth" (Revelation
11:3).

Before many of the judgments plague our planet, God
chose a pair of choice servants to preach to the citizens of earth.
These may have been the men who converted the 144,000 Jewish evangelists. Who were these powerful prophets? This question has created debate among students of prophecy for years. I
believe the Scriptures point to two men: one of these witnesses
is Elijah the prophet. The first reason I believe this to be true is

that Malachi the prophet predicted that Elijah would come to prepare the way for the Messiah (Malachi 3:1–3; 4:5–6).

Second, Elijah never experienced death; therefore, he could return and die, just as the witnesses do.

Third, the witnesses have the same sign that was given to Elijah in regard to rain. "These men have power to shut up the sky so that it will not rain during the time they are prophesying" (Revelation 11:6).

Fourth, Elijah was one of the two who appeared at the Transfiguration (Matthew 17:3), when the death of Christ was discussed.

I believe the other witness will be Moses. He, also, appeared at the Transfiguration. He turned waters into blood, just as the witnesses will do (Exodus 7:19–20; Revelation 11:6). Also, the body of Moses was preserved by God so that he might be restored.

Tourists often ask their Israeli or Arab Holy Land guides, "Where is Moses buried?" No one knows. If his grave site were known, the Jews would have a shrine built over it larger than any other in the land. But Moses does not have a grave.

Moses and Elijah—mighty men of old, and mighty men of the future!

Power of the Two Witnesses

For three and a half years, these men are invincible. They will stop the rain, turn the waters to blood, and strike the earth with plagues. They will tell men to their faces about their human wickedness; they will stab hearts with warnings of future judgments, even worse than the past. The hatred this pair arouses will be intense. After hearing them, no one will shake their hands and say, "That was a very inspiring sermon, pastor"!

Some will repent, but many will be aroused to a frenzy of hatred. When their work is finished, the order will be given for the two witnesses to be killed. On stage bolts the new ruler,

". . . the beast that comes up from the Abyss" (Revelation 11:7). This is the first of thirty-six references to the Beast in Revelation, and apparently his killing the witnesses is the first great act that he will use to gain a following. The frenzied mob will cheer the executions.

What a great illustration of this truth: "The man of God in the will of God is immortal until he has finished the work God has given him to do." God will not allow these two men to be killed until He says the word.

For three and a half days, their bodies will be displayed on a street in Jerusalem. We are told that during this time men from "every people, tribe, language and nation will gaze on their bodies and refuse them burial" (Revelation 11:9).

For years, the critics have laughed at this "impossible" prediction. Now, with the advance of satellite television, no one can scoff at the possibility.

Celebration of Death

A ghoulish display of the prophets' bodies is not enough; the crowd turns their deaths into a holiday. They send each other gifts, rejoicing in the demise of these tormenting preachers. It will be a counterfeit Christmas.

In the midst of the jubilation, the laughter ends, the cheers cease. People are frozen with fear as they hear a voice from heaven calling to the prophets to "Come up here." Life is breathed into them and they ascend to heaven in a cloud, ". . . while their enemies looked on" (11:12). The dread this will cause is hard to describe.

Meanwhile, back in the executive suite, the Beast will attempt to explain the translation of the prisoners he killed, but he will not be able to duplicate this miracle.

Divine Retribution

As the two witnesses are raptured and the world recoils in fear, there is an earthquake. Seven thousand men, leaders in the city, are killed. Those who are left alive call to God in terror, but not in repentance. Hearts may be pounding in fear, but not breaking under conviction.

During the last period of three and a half years, Jerusalem will see nothing but war; one Gentile army after another will invade the city and march up and down its streets. The Great Tribulation begins.

Sound the Last Trumpet

Soon John will introduce us to some of the leading characters in this dark drama, but first we have another preview of coming attractions—this time it's a coronation which will officially crown the Lord of lords and King of kings. This celebration will not take place until God has defeated all His enemies at the Battle of Armageddon.

The seventh trumpet sounds and the twenty-four elders leave their thrones and fall down to worship God. These men represent the redeemed of all ages and they rejoice because they see their King beginning to reign. The elders worshiped God at the beginning of the judgments (Revelation 5:8–10) and now they worship Him at the end of judgment. They will be a part of that great chorus that inspired Handel: ". . . and he will reign for ever and ever" (Revelation 11:15). I've never been able to hear that without adding, "Hallelujah, hallelujah."

Four major events are mentioned when the last trumpet sounds. First, the nations of the world are angry. This fury is described by Warren Wiersbe:

"Note the change in attitude shown by the nations of the world. In Revelation 11:2, the nations ruthlessly take over Jerusalem. In 11:9, they rejoice at the death of the two witnesses. But now, they are angry; their arrogance and joy did not last very long. This belligerent attitude finally will cause the nations to unite to fight God at the great battle of Armageddon."[4]

The second event is God's judgment of the dead. This is one event that is clearly indicated on the prophetic calendar. It is called the Great White Throne judgment, and if you are a believer in Jesus Christ your name will not be on the docket.

The believers of the Old Testament—and those who became believers during the Tribulation—will become part of the third event, which are rewards at the end of the Tribulation. Church age believers received their rewards at the judgment seat of Christ soon after the Rapture.

Fourth, God will destroy those who destroy the earth (Revelation 11:18). Those who have followed the destroyer (and we know his identity), are called the destroyers of the earth.

Return of the Lost Ark

The ark of the Old Testament disappeared during the Exile, and it has never been found, in spite of Hollywood's fantasy adventures. When John is given a view of the temple in heaven and the elders worshiping God, the ark is seen returned to its sanctuary. This vision would greatly encourage the suffering people to whom John sent this amazing book, for the ark stood for the presence and protection of God.

Someday the lost ark will be returned to its proper place. Jews everywhere, take note: War on earth can never remove or destroy His protection.

13

WAR IN
HEAVEN

December 7, 1941. The Japanese bombed Pearl Harbor
and the war in the Pacific headlined onto the world scene.
America was caught with weak defenses and shocked citizens.
In July of that fateful year, General Douglas MacArthur wrote,
"We began an eleventh-hour struggle to build up enough force
to repel an enemy . . . Washington had come to realize the
danger too late."[1]

Within seventy-two hours after Pearl Harbor, the FBI
sprung into action. Thousands of "suspicious enemy aliens"
were arrested, many of whom were interned without cause. But
espionage is an insidious weapon and every precaution needed
to be taken for the national safety. In the following months, an
underground war was waged against spy rings in this country
and abroad. Many war plants might have exploded and the
coastal cities of America could have been invaded if we had not
uncovered the enemy's strategy.

Know your enemy. In spiritual conflicts, we must know
and understand our adversary, or we'll be the victims of

surprise attacks. Most of us do not realize that while we may be able to see the threat from earthly enemies, there is an unseen warfare being waged in the heavenlies. In the war of the universe, good and evil struggle for supremacy.

In chapter twelve of Revelation, we are spectators who watch the war between God and Satan and their heavenly armies. We also meet some leading characters in this great global conflict.

First, we are introduced to a woman—who is not a woman at all.

The Great Wonder-Woman

"A great and wondrous sign appeared in heaven: a woman clothed with the sun, with the moon under her feet and a crown of twelve stars on her head. She was pregnant and cried out in pain as she was about to give birth" (Revelation 12:1, 2).

Who is she?

The Christian Scientists say she is Mary Baker Glover Patterson Eddy, and the male child she bore was the Christian Scientist movement. Mary Baker says the dragon is the mortal mind that is ready to devour the teaching set forth in *Science and Health.* This view has absolutely no basis in Scripture.

The Roman Catholic church says that the woman is Mary, the mother of our Lord. A Spanish artist named Murillo painted some famous pictures to prove Mary was this woman. One of the paintings showed her great with child and portrayed her assumption into heaven. Two things are wrong with his portrayal: first, Mary did not have an assumption into heaven; second, why would she be shown pregnant in heaven after Jesus had already been born, resurrected, and Himself ascended into heaven?

Some Protestants say this is a picture of the church. However, the church did not give birth to Christ, Christ gave birth to the church.

I believe the Bible clearly identifies this "woman" as Israel, whom "an enormous red dragon," representing Satan, seeks to destroy. This woman (symbolically) gives us the answer to why anti-Semitism has been one of the dirtiest blots on the pages of man's existence.

The woman (Israel) is described ". . . clothed with the sun, with the moon under her feet and a crown of twelve stars on her head" (Revelation 12:1).

This clothing was described in the Old Testament story of Joseph. In Genesis 37, he had a dream where he saw the sun, moon, and eleven stars bowing down before him. The sun represented his father, Jacob; the moon symbolized his mother, Rachel; the eleven stars were his brothers—remember the fellows who threw him down a well and sold him into slavery?

Joseph's dream *did* come true and from this symbolization we can deduce that the woman was Israel and the twelve tribes, founders of her race.

This woman has a child: "She gave birth to a son, a male child, who will rule all the nations with an iron scepter. And her child was snatched up to God and to his throne" (Revelation 12:5).

The identification of the child could not be clearer, even in symbolic terms. Christ was born, He was resurrected, and when He comes again He will rule the nations with a rod of iron. The actual fulfillment of the last part of this prophecy does not come until we reach the end of Revelation.

The woman, the nation of Israel, and the Jewish people, have an implacable enemy. The greatest anti-Semite of all time is the second character in this scene.

The Enormous Dragon

Now we know where people get the idea that Satan dresses in red and sports a long tail and horns. That's not true, costume manufacturers and kids at Halloween to the contrary.

When John saw the sign of this "enormous red dragon," the picture was not a photograph of how he looks, but a symbolic representation of his cruel, vile nature. His color is red, for his path has always been covered with blood and death. He is a seven-headed monster; the number seven signifies totality and the head conveys the idea of intelligence, with an IQ that goes off the chart. He is so clever that he can pull the wool over a person's eyes, blinding him to the truth. Paul warned the Corinthians about this strategy: "If the Good News we preach is hidden to anyone, it is hidden from the one who is on the road to eternal death. Satan, who is the god of this evil world, has made him blind, unable to see the glorious light of the Gospel that is shining upon him, or to understand the amazing message we preach about the glory of Christ, who is God" (2 Corinthians 4:3, 4, TLB).

Satan can transform himself into an angel of light. His greatest disguise is Mr. Nice Guy.

The beast had "ten horns." The significance of this in light of prophecy is vitally important in this present age. We'll find out more about these horns in the next chapter.

Motivated to Murder

"The dragon stood in front of the woman who was about to give birth, so that he might devour her child the moment it was born" (Revelation 12:4).

Satan heard God in the Garden of Eden when he was told that the seed of woman would crush his head. From that day on, Satan has been trying to destroy the promised seed.

He motivated Cain to kill Abel, but God raised up Seth to carry the seed. Satan caused such evil in the world that God destroyed the earth by means of a flood, but God saved Noah and his family. Satan motivated Esau in an attempt to kill Jacob, but God preserved Jacob. Satan moved Pharaoh to destroy all the male children of the Hebrew families, but God saved Moses.

At other times in Israel's history, Satan tried to kill all the Jews so the Messiah could not be born. When Jesus was actually born, Satan, motivated to murder again, caused Herod to slay all the babies in Bethlehem, but an angel warned Joseph to take Jesus and escape to Egypt. The maniac murderer was thwarted again.

On a Friday afternoon at three o'clock, the day before Passover, Satan thought he had achieved the triumph he had been seeking throughout history. When the broken body of our Lord was wrapped in linen, embalmed with spices, and sealed in a tomb, Satan gloried in his success. But God never changes His purposes. He planned for this Jesus of Nazareth to rule the nations with a rod of iron, and God took Him up to His throne in glory. Satan's defeat turned to God's triumph.

The Wrath of the Dragon

When Satan saw the resurrection of Jesus, he did not have an Easter celebration. He turned his fury upon the body of Christ, the church. Satan had those who preached the gospel of Jesus Christ—the apostles, missionaries, evangelists—crucified, sawed in pieces, fed to the wild beasts, while sneering emperors watched the sport. Edicts were sent from Rome to destroy the Christians from the face of the earth.

Paganism was replaced by papal authority. It is estimated that more than fifty million Christians laid down their lives in fire and blood before the Inquisition of Papal Rome. This is the wrath of the dragon against the people of the Lord!

Anti-Semitism has its roots in the mind of Satan, for Israel and the Jewish race were responsible for his defeat at the cross.

I believe God has a special place in His kingdom for those who have cared for the Jewish people, even in their unbelief. I remember the story of Casper ten Boom, patriarchal father of Corrie, who said, as he was arrested in his home and watch shop in Haarlem, Holland, for the crime of hiding Jews from the Gestapo, "If I die in prison, it will be an honor to have given my life for God's ancient people."

The Great Unseen War

Satan finds it hard to give up. He makes one last attempt to take over heaven, but God has a strong general in the person of Michael, His archangel. Satan and the black angels line up against Michael and his white angels in a strategic battle. This unseen war is not discussed in detail in Revelation; however, we learn there are spiritual forces at work that we cannot comprehend.

The role of the evil angels is to help Satan run this world. Satan's mafia is organized to control the world behind the scenes. This is what Paul was telling the Ephesians: "For our struggle is not against flesh and blood, but against the rulers, against the authorities, against the owners of this dark world and against the spiritual forces of evil in the heavenly realms" (Ephesians 6:12).

Evil is not abstract. An intelligent being is the source of evil and he assigns the administration of his works to real angelic creatures.

Daniel was one character who described the effect of angelic conflict on his life. He had been praying for three weeks when he had a vision of a heavenly visitor. This angel, probably Gabriel, told Daniel that his prayer had been heard from the very first day he uttered it. If I had been Daniel, I probably would have said, "Then why did you make me pray for twenty-one days? That's pretty tiring, you know."

Gabriel explained that he had been detained in his special-delivery prayer answer because he had been in a war with the Prince of Persia. Fortunately, one of God's strong men, Michael, was sent from heaven to help out Gabriel, so he was able to continue his mission to deliver Daniel's prayer request.

This Prince of Persia was no pussy-cat. Satan knows he has to get to rulers, heads of organizations, and the influence-peddlers to carry out his plans.

In his classic book on demonology, Dr. Merrill Unger wrote:

> History since the fall of man, has been an unbroken attestation of the ominous fact of evil powers in human rulers. . . . perhaps the most solemn demonstration of the utter barbarity and horrible cruelty and wickedness of men energized by demon power, has been reserved for the boasted civilization and enlightenment of the 20th century.
>
> Hitler, the demon-energized and demon-directed scourge of Europe has come and gone, leaving behind a trail of agonized suffering and a stage of chaos upon which atheistic communism is determined to perpetrate even greater evils.[2]

The Voyager 2 spacecraft has relayed photographs to earth, causing scientists to revel in their excitement over the findings. The data sent made this spacecraft the unchallenged leader among planetary explorers, at least until now. Space also contains unseen armies that no marvel of scientific achievement can discern. It may be eerie to think about, but we should be grateful that God has His angels watching over us to challenge, and eventually defeat, Satan's malevolent troops.

But Wasn't Satan Judged at the Cross?

Of course he was. Christ did the work at the cross. Why, then, does Satan seem to be winning? The homes of our nations are rapidly deteriorating, our national morality is on the decline, the church is weak. Visit the classrooms where our young people are being educated and wonder how God has any influence. Our inner cities are crawling with vice. If Satan is judged, who's doing all his work?

I read about Robinson Crusoe, trying to teach his man Friday the doctrines of the Christian faith. When he came to explaining the devil, he told Friday that the devil was the enemy of God and that he was trying to defeat the purposes of God in the world.

Friday asked, "Is God not strong as devil?"

"Of course, God is stronger," Crusoe answered. "Christians pray to God for victory over the devil."

Friday puzzled about that one. "But why God no kill devil so make him no more do wicked?"

Just as we do when our kids ask us questions we don't know quite how to answer, Crusoe pretended he didn't hear, hoping Friday would forget the question.

Friday persisted and finally Crusoe gave up and answered, "Well, God will punish the devil in the end."

"But why God not kill devil now?"

We may not use fractured English, but our question is the same. "If Satan was judged at the cross, why isn't there more victory over him here and now?"

Legally, Calvary was Satan's undoing. All his hopes were canceled when the Lord Jesus died and rose again. However, like any other legal action, the decision must be enforced. The concept of enforcement is illustrated in our own government. We know the federal government has three branches: the legislative branch, or Congress, passes the laws; the judicial branch, the Supreme Court, interprets the laws; the executive branch, centered in the president, enforces the laws.

History gives us a good example of this principle. The eighteenth amendment said that the manufacture, sale, or transportation of liquor was illegal. It was the law of the land, having been passed by Congress. But its enforcement was left in the hands of a man named Andrew Mellon, who was secretary of the treasury. He was also the head of one of the largest brewery syndicates in the world. Interesting predicament. The law became useless, because it was not enforced.

Satan was judged at the cross, and the enforcement of that judgment is now in the hands of the church of Jesus Christ. The tool that enforces Satan's defeat is the tool of prayer. Remember our friend Daniel? He prayed for twenty-one days and finally the angel of Satan was defeated.

It is prayer in the name of Jesus that is the effective weapon for changing men and nations in the world. Earthly victories depend upon heavenly victories. The ultimate victory over Satan is in the future, but we can enforce it now through the most powerful weapon Christians have—prayer.[3]

Satan Crashes

Satan and his angels are kicked out of heaven and his downward path begins. From heaven to earth—from earth to the bottomless pit—from the bottomless pit to the lake of fire and brimstone. When this maniac of many disguises is hurled to earth, three things happen. First (and we can understand this), there is praise in heaven. Satan can no longer accuse the believers before God.

Did you know that he sits in heaven accusing us? "Oh, by the way, God, did you notice David Jeremiah down there in California? He really blew it today in his so-called Christian life. Just thought you'd like to know."

No sooner does the prosecutor make his accusation, than our personal lawyer, our advocate Jesus Christ, steps to the front of the courtroom and says, "You don't have anything against Jeremiah. I paid the penalty for his sins upon the cross, so drop this case for lack of evidence."

Satan's ouster from heaven will take place on a future day, at the half-way point in the Tribulation.

When he hits Earth, he's in a blazing fury ". . . because he knows that his time is short" (Revelation 12:12). He doesn't have much time left to destroy the believing remnant in Israel, so he unleashes everything he has. This is the last wave of anti-Semitism that will roll over the world. Satan wants to destroy the nation of Israel, particularly as the time draws near for the Messiah to return to earth to establish the promised kingdom.

The dragon is especially angry with those within the nation of Israel "who obey God's commandments and hold to the testimony of Jesus" (Revelation 12:17). This is not a reference to Jews in general, but rather to Jewish believers.

Israel Airlift

Believing Jews are going to experience supernatural provision in that future day, just as they did when the Lord guided them in the wilderness. The Bible says, "The woman was given the two wings of a great eagle" (12:14), which could mean aircraft, unknown to first-century John. For three and a half years this group of Jewish believers will be protected some place in the desert. Some Bible scholars believe this could be in Petra, a natural ancient fortress in the southern desert of Jordan.

Isn't it possible that the "eagle" could refer to the United States? This is sheer supposition, but I would like to think that our air force will save those believers.

The Antichrist, indwelt by Satan, is going to be furious that the believers have escaped his grasp, so he will send his henchmen after them, like a flood. However, God will cause the earth to swallow up the advancing troops and protect His own children.

The Antichrist will be so enraged at this counteroffensive that he will unleash his bloodiest attacks on remaining believers. Satan seems to be winning the war at times, but his doom is settled and his defeat is certain.

Is this man, the Antichrist, alive today? Is he a child, raised to hate, or a teenager, inspired by power? Is he in a position of political influence right now, just waiting for the opportunity to step onto the world scene with his solutions to global problems?

Let's see what sort of a fellow he will be as Revelation writes a biohistory of him. He is a man more likely to be wearing a custom-made business suit than horns and a tail; he will be a real man, possessed with charismatic authority— the world's greatest megalomaniac.

14

MALICIOUS MASQUERADE

The world will go into shock. Men and women will freeze
in unbelief as the global media shout the incredible news.

PRESIDENT SHOT

ASSASSIN KILLS JUDAS CHRISTOPHER

U. S. OF EUROPE MOURNS LOSS OF LEADER

Christopher was pronounced dead on arrival at the International Hospital of Rome this morning. The motorcade of
U.S.E. officials was traveling along the Via Veneto when the
president was hit in the temple by a single bullet. He slumped
in his seat in full view of his cabinet officials and millions
watching on interglobal satellite.

Christopher has been hailed by leaders of every country as
the greatest world figure in history. He was widely acclaimed as
the most brilliant politician of the Second Millennium.

The loss in world leadership cannot be measured. No
other man has done more to solve the problems of the world
and unify nations.

For three days there will be no other story in the news. The countries of the world will be in chaos, wondering how they can find another man to guide them through the perilous times.

As his body lies in state in the capitol rotunda of the United States of Europe, the television networks will preempt every program to cover this one event. Surrounding the coffin will be the governors of the ten European states, the president and all members of Congress from the United States of America, and the leading officials of every other country. Most of them will stand frozen with grief, and many will be openly weeping.

Suddenly, the body of Judas Christopher stirs. He sits up. Slowly, he rises from his casket and walks to the nearest microphone. A gasp of disbelief is heard in the room. Then he speaks, his resonant voice reassuring everyone that he has truly been resurrected.

"Do not fear, my friends, I am alive. Look at me—three days ago I had a bullet hole in my head. As you can see, I'm completely whole. My greatest wish now is to continue with the unification of nations and religions. To bring together people of all colors and faith into peaceful coexistence. I shall have one world, based upon love and mutual respect."

And the world headlines will scream:

HE IS ALIVE!

A STUNNED WORLD WATCHES AS CHRISTOPHER
IS RESURRECTED!

PLEDGES TO WORK FOR WORLD PEACE

Truth Will Be Stranger Than Fiction

We don't know exactly how it will happen, but someday the man who has been indwelt by Satan himself, the one who is the great counterfeiter, will pull his greatest masquerade. He will have a fatal wound, and, as the whole world mourns, he will be healed. His leadership will be established without question. Every earthly inhabitant, except the believers whose names are written in the Book of Life, will worship him.

He will be handsome and charismatic, able to sway the masses to perform his satanic bidding. Daniel described him as, ". . . more imposing than the others and that had eyes and mouth that spoke boastfully" (Daniel 7:20).

Daniel also wrote that he has "the eyes of a man," indicating that he will be brilliant (Daniel 7:8).

He will command a cultic worship that will make Joseph Smith and Jim Jones look like boy scout leaders. "He will oppose and will exalt himself over everything that is called God or worshiped, so that he sets himself up in God's temple, proclaiming himself to be God" (2 Thessalonians 2:4).

For a time at the beginning of the Tribulation, it will seem like the Antichrist is a brilliant and benevolent dictator. As his true character emerges, his ability to sway the masses will increase.

I can remember hearing recordings of the voice of Hitler as he spoke to the people of Berlin. At first you would strain to hear what he was saying. Starting in a beguiling whisper, he would gradually become louder and more strident. Before he finished, he would be shrieking insanely and the German masses would return his rhetoric with shouts of "Heil, Hitler."

Antichrist will be a Hitler with infinitely more evil power.

John Saw Him Rise from the Sea

In Revelation 13, John saw "a beast coming out of the sea. He had ten horns and seven heads, with ten crowns on his horns, and on each head a blasphemous name" (13:1).

He appeared to John, just as Daniel had described it over 600 years earlier, as a beast resembling a lion, a bear, a leopard, and a fourth, unnamed beast with power which surpassed its predecessors. This beast represented the four kingdoms that would arise one after another: Babylon, Medo-Persia, Greece, and Rome. The prediction of the rise and fall of these four empires was fulfilled with complete accuracy.

John said this beast resembled a leopard. It may not be a coincidence that a leopard, with its colors of brown, black, and white, is one beast that represents the three major races. The Antichrist will be the Universal Man, the leader who can unify the world.

There have been many guesses about the identity of the Antichrist. In the *Edinburgh Encyclopedia,* fourteen different people were listed as this man. Some of our greatest Christian leaders, such as Wycliffe, Huss, and Luther, thought the Pope was the Antichrist. Hitler, Moshe Dayan, John F. Kennedy, and Henry Kissinger, had the dubious distinctions of being called by that infamous name. Some people recently have added Mikhail Gorbachev to the list.

He may be alive today, living in relative obscurity, but he certainly has not appeared on the scene yet. He will come out of the Fourth Empire (the Revived Roman Empire), which is rapidly being formed in our time.

Unified Europe in 1992

The vision of 1992 and the European Community, or Common Market, is accelerating in both excitement and apprehension throughout the world. When the twelve nations which are now committed to unity emerge as one powerful bloc, the market, with a population of 320 million, will be as large as the United States and Japan combined.

"Europhoria" describes the attitude of many Europeans toward the new political union. In Brussels, the "Eurocapital," there are Euro-schools, Euro-consultants, and shops that sell Euro-gadgets. Along with the exhilaration will come the obstacles, the patriots of each country who will suffer from a loss of pride and income.

Newsweek said, "The path to a single market will be paved

with sloppy compromises and missed deadlines. Inevitably, though, a Europe without internal borders will emerge. Europe's economies need it to compete and survive. And it is the absolute pre-condition for accomplishing the long-term European dream: a real political union that will restore Europe to its role as a world power."[1]

In the book *Megatrends 2000* the authors wrote about the expected global economic boom of the 1990s and concluded, ". . . 1992 is an extraordinary phenomenon. Nothing like it has ever before been tried in history. . . . The excitement in Western European government and business circles is almost euphoric. The process is now irreversible. It is unstoppable."[2]

A world power will need a strong leader, especially as the problems of population, environment, economics, and animosities increase. We should not leap to the conclusion that the first head of a united Europe will be the Antichrist. Believers will be raptured before he is revealed. However, we see the ground being prepared for him now.

The Bible indicates this Revived Roman Empire will have ten heads, and yet the European Common Market has twelve countries at this time. It does not matter how many there are now, the time will come when there will be just ten. God's Word is inerrantly accurate.

Demon on a Leash

The Antichrist will be a demon with a body, an intellect, and a personality. He will be living on borrowed time, loaned to him by God. Notice how he received his diabolical traits:

"The beast *was given* a mouth to utter proud words and blasphemies and to exercise his authority for forty-two months . . . *He was given* power to make war against the saints and to conquer them. *He was given* authority over every tribe, people, language and nation" (Revelation 13:5, 7).

God allows the Antichrist to have this power, but he has him on a leash. His doom is foreordained.

The Second Beast

"Then I saw another beast, coming out of the earth. He had two horns like a lamb, but he spoke like a dragon. He exercised all the authority of the first beast on his behalf, and made the earth and its inhabitants worship the first beast, whose fatal wound had been healed" (Revelation 13:11).

This beast is the false prophet, the right-hand man for the Antichrist. How clever Satan is to continue this malicious masquerade and complete the unholy trinity. Just as God is a trinity, so is Satan. His program is a total counterfeit of God's program. Satan's answer to God the Son is the Antichrist. The Holy Spirit's counterfeit is the second beast, or the False Prophet.

The Holy Spirit has one main objective, and that is to glorify Jesus Christ. The False Prophet has one objective, and that is to cause people to worship the first beast.

It may seem strange to see a religious leader as a key player during the Tribulation, but this has been the pattern throughout history. Man needs a religious source. Naisbitt said, "Religious belief is intensifying worldwide under the gravitational pull of the year 2000, the millennium."[3]

The longing in men's hearts for a belief system is universal; even atheism and materialism are religions.

The False Prophet will use all types of religious props to deceive people. Today, we see the satanical influence of counterfeit Christianity enticing people into its web. A friend was telling me about a conversation with a woman who said she speaks on a regular basis with the apostle John. This woman said she was listening to the radio one night around midnight, and the apostle John was talking. She was instructed to call a certain phone number, which she did. After that, John spoke to her through a channeler, a "very intelligent professional gentleman in his middle 40s," whose message was one of pure love.

I wonder what that woman would think about John's message in the book of Revelation?

Linda Evans, a television star who is called one of the world's most beautiful women, believes that her emotional security and sense of peace rests in the hands of a "channeler."

She said, "I've tried a lot of things along the way—psychiatry, TM, Science of Mind. I don't know yet where the answer is. . . ."⁴

Religion without Jesus is the tool of Satan to draw people into his realm. During the Tribulation, religiosity will be intense and the False Prophet will use every counterfeit tool in his arsenal.

Satanic Sign Language

The False Prophet will have the power to perform great miracles. ". . . even causing fire to come down from heaven to earth in full view of men" (13:13).

Imagine the astonishment of all on earth as great streaks of fire blaze across the sky. Perhaps it will be a part of a gigantic celebration for the Antichrist. This spectacular show may be to center attention on Jerusalem, where the image of the beast will be exhibited. The flaming display is not unlike God's miraculous work. He called down fire upon Sodom and Gomorrah; Elijah brought down fire from heaven on Mount Carmel. We were told in Revelation 11 that if anyone tries to harm the two witnesses, fire comes from their mouths and destroys their enemies.

God has often revealed Himself by fire, and the deceiving false prophet will do the same.

The Talking Statue

The false prophet will have a special building project planned to erect a statue of the Antichrist in the rebuilt Jerusalem Temple. There will be no need for an all-member canvas or pledges from the faithful. When the Antichrist recovers from his fatal wound and becomes the proclaimed world leader, his followers will worship him.

No sculptor in any age of man has formed a statue like this one will be. The image of the Antichrist will speak and issue a decree that anyone who refuses to fall down and worship it will be killed.

We don't know how this evil magic will be performed, but it is another evidence of the power of demons that will prevail in those days.

"Because of the signs he was given power to do on behalf of the first beast, he deceived the inhabitants of the earth. He ordered them to set up an image in honor of the beast who was wounded by the sword and yet lived. He was given power to give breath to the image of the first beast, so that it could speak and cause all who refused to worship the image to be killed" (Revelation 13:14, 15).

The setting up of the image of the beast is evidently what Jesus had in mind when He said in His Olivet discourse: "So when you see standing in the holy place '*the abomination* that causes desolation,' spoken of through the prophet Daniel—let the reader understand—then let those who are in Judea flee to the mountains" (Matthew 24:15, 16, emphasis added).

The View from Heaven

If we are able to pull the door of heaven open a crack and see what is happening on earth, we would see the followers of the Antichrist prostrating themselves before the altar of his statue, while we are worshiping Christ in all His glory at heaven's altar.

Below us we might see the lines forming for the seal to be placed on each person's right hand or forehead. Everyone files past the False Prophet and his appointed ministers and has 666 stamped on his skin.

God also has sealed ones—remember the seal on the fore-heads of the 144,000 Jewish evangelists? Again, Satan has coun-terfeited God's work.

Branded by the Beast

During World War II it was necessary to have stamps or a card to buy certain food. Gasoline was scarce, and many other goods were in short supply. In America the hardships were minor, for the winning of the war was a national effort, but rationing was a way of life.

During the Tribulation, there will be no surge of patrio-tism. It will be moment-by-moment survival. The law of the beast will be, "Worship me or starve."

Why 666?

Why is the mark of the beast 666? Superstitions about this number and its meaning could fill volumes. Here are some interesting things about it: Goliath was six cubits in height, his spear's head weighed six shekels and he had six pieces of armor. Nebuchadnezzar's image was sixty cubits in height, and six cubits wide.

Man was created on the sixth day. He has to work six of seven days. A Hebrew slave could not be a slave more than six years. The fields of the Jews could not be sown for more than six years running.

The most logical explanation for the mark is that the number six in the Bible is the number of man. The beast repre-sents the ultimate in human ingenuity and cleverness.

Something Is Missing

The children of the great composer, Bach, found that the easiest way to awaken their father was to play a few lines of music and leave off the last note. Bach would get up immediately, go to the piano and strike the final chord.

Donald Grey Barnhouse told how he awoke one morning during the Christmas season, went to the piano and played "Silent Night," purposely stopping before striking the last note. He walked into the hallway and listened to the sounds from the children's rooms upstairs. His eight-year-old son had stopped reading and was trying to find the final note on his harmonica. Another one of the children was singing the last note with great volume. His wife called, "Donald, did you do that on purpose?"

Human nature demands the completion of the last note. The number 666 reminds us that something is missing. That missing something is Someone. He is a seven, and that is the complete number.

God has His seven-headed Lamb of God, the second person of the Trinity. He has His seven spirits of God, the third person of the trinity. And He has His saints singing the sevenfold doxology.

Satan has his six . . . but God is seven. The old counterfeiter will never be able to fool all of the people all of the time, only some. . . .

15

EMPIRES OF
THE BEAST

This is a tale of two Babylons, one mystical and one material. Babylon—wealthy, intriguing, and immoral—is mentioned more times in the Bible than any other city, with the exception of Jerusalem. The first great empire of the Gentile world, it was the home of Nebuchadnezzar, the most influential king on earth at that time. Within its hundred-feet-high walls, so thick that four chariots could race abreast atop them, the Jews had languished as captives for seventy years. Babylon represents what man can do without God; it is a picture today of the Western world, with all our learning and science, building "our Babylon" without the direction and inspiration of God.

When John was given a vision of the world tomorrow where the beast would reign, he saw that this world leader would be supported by two powerful global allies: one will be religious in nature and the other, economic. This unholy alliance will form the final world government—doomed for extinction.

The beast uses three cities in his reign upon the earth. He

will begin in Rome (as head of the Revived Roman Empire); then he will jet to Jerusalem to carry out his plan for the Jews (establishing himself as the Supreme High Commander); finally, he will move his command base to "Babylon," the economic and political hub of his empire.

Mystery Babylon

John is shown a picture of a woman, who was so despicable that in his prophetic vision, he was "greatly astonished." It must have taken a real shocker to jolt him once again. Who is this vile woman? Trying to understand her identity will help us understand how much of what is called "religion" in the world today is a crimson path to spiritual destruction.

> One of the seven angels who had the seven bowls came and said to me, "Come, I will show you the punishment of the great prostitute, who sits on many waters. With her the kings of the earth committed adultery and inhabitants of the earth were intoxicated with the wine of her adulteries. Then the angel carried me away in the Spirit into a desert. There I saw a woman sitting on a scarlet beast that was covered with blasphemous names and had seven heads and ten horns. The woman was dressed in purple and scarlet, and was glittering with gold, precious stones and pearls. She held a golden cup in her hand, filled with abominable things and the filth of her adulteries." This title was written on her forehead:
>
>
>
> MYSTERY
> BABYLON THE GREAT
> THE MOTHER OF PROSTITUTES
> AND OF THE ABOMINATIONS OF THE EARTH.
>
>
>
> I saw that the woman was drunk with the blood of the saints, the blood of those who bore testimony to Jesus (Revelation 17:1–6).

Born in Babylon

A false religious system was born on the plains of Shinar in ancient Babylon, where the first world dictator, Nimrod, defying God, built a tower that would reach to heaven. This tower was used for studying the stars and established the basis for astrology. From the very beginning, Babylon was associated with sorcery and astrology.

Out of Babylon came another movement, promoted by Nimrod's wife, Semiramis, the first high priestess of idolatry. According to legend, she had a son by the name of Tammuz, who was conceived miraculously by a sunbeam (true legend). When Tammuz grew up, he was killed by a wild boar, but after forty days of his mother's weeping, he was raised from the dead. It was in this story of Semiramis and Tammuz that the cultic worship of "the mother and child" began to be spread throughout the world. The liturgy of worship was defined, as the mother was identified as "queen of heaven" (Jeremiah 44:15–19).

Forty days of Lent memorialized the forty days of weeping over the death of Tammuz, and at the end of the forty days, the feast of Ishtar was observed to celebrate the resurrection of Tammuz. Part of the celebration of Ishtar was the exchanging of Ishtar eggs, symbolizing new life. Believe it or not, the term "Easter" is derived from the word "Ishtar."

The prophet Ezekiel was called by the Lord to go to the temple and see this cultic practice in process. Ezekiel watched the women of Israel observing the forty days of Lent for the slaying of the pagan, Tammuz. The Lord called this an abomination (Ezekiel 8:13–14).

The mother-son cult finally ended in Rome, where the Roman emperor was elected Pontifex Maximus (the greatest high priest). When the Roman emperor was gone, the Bishop of Rome assumed all of his titles and responsibilities; today he is known as the Pope.

A great Bible scholar, Dr. H. A. Ironside, wrote:

When Constantine came to the throne and the first pope assumed the title Pontifex Maximus, all those heathen associations and ceremonies that had their beginning with Nimrod—the worship of the Queen of the Heavens, the eating of the wafer, the doctrine of purgatory, the wearing of vestments, and the observance of a thousand and one lesser mysteries—all these were brought into the church, and for a thousand years they prevailed over all Europe. Thus the Roman Catholic Church with all its doctrines and practices came into existence.[1]

There is no such thing in the Bible as the worship of a female deity, and Mary was never presented as anything other than the humble servant of God who was chosen as the virgin to bear Jesus Christ.

Many Paths to Mystical Babylon

When Daniel walked into Babylon, he encountered more than a lion's den. In King Nebuchadnezzar's court, a motley crew of magicians, astrologers, and sorcerers hovered around to interpret dreams, calling upon their spirit guides and charting the signs in the stars. Does this sound familiar? We're living in Nebuchadnezzar's courtyard of cults and the occult today.

Not all of Babylon the Great is occult; much of its influence is in the watered-down religion of liberal churches and parachurch organizations which profess to be Christian, but deny many of the basic doctrines of the Bible. (Remember the lukewarm church at Laodecia?)

This is the type of church which will be in existence at the time of the return of Christ, and it is here today.

The Great Whore

No respectable woman wants to be called such a name, but the woman in Revelation 17 is no lady. The Greek word for "whore" is the word *porne,* which is usually translated in the New Testament by the word "harlot."

Dr. John Walvoord helps us understand the use of such a vile description for the end-time church:

The picture of the woman as utterly evil signifies spiritual adultery, portraying those who outwardly and religiously seem to be joined to the true God, but who are untrue to this relationship. The symbolism of spiritual adultery is not ordinarily used of heathen nations who know not God, but always of people who outwardly carry the name of God while actually worshipping and serving other gods . . . In the New Testament, the church is viewed as a virgin destined to be joined to her husband in the future (2 Corinthians 11:2), but she is warned against spiritual adultery (James 4:4).[2]

In evangelical churches today, no matter how positive the messages may be, without the foundation of Bible teaching those churches are committing spiritual adultery.

Two-Faced Woman

The prostitute of the end times has two faces: apostasy and religion. This was predicted almost 2,000 years ago: "The Spirit clearly says that in later times some will abandon the faith and follow deceiving spirits and things taught by demons. Such teachings come through hypocritical liars, whose consciences have been seared as with a hot iron" (1 Timothy 4:1, 2).

Apostasy is happening all around us. Pulpits, radio, television, seminaries, abound in false doctrines. The Christian scholar, Francis Shaeffer, said, "We must not forget that the world is on fire. We live in the post-Christian world which is under the judgment of God."[3]

Why are the teachers of false doctrine so successful? The apostle Paul said: "For the time will come when men will not put up with sound doctrine. Instead, to suit their own desires, they will gather around them a great number of teachers to say what their itching ears want to hear. They will turn their ears away from the truth and turn aside to myths" (2 Timothy 4:3, 4).

This is what apostasy is all about: forsaking the true meaning of biblical doctrine or choosing which doctrines to believe and which to discard.

Foreshadows of this one-world religious system can be seen in the two faces of Mystery Babylon: first, the lukewarm and apostate church, and second, the drug-filled, occult-influenced millions who follow "deceiving spirits."

New Age and Mystery Babylon

Many people today, dissatisfied with the weak spiritual temperature of the Western church, have turned for answers to the New Age movement that does not ignore God, but claims that all religions are one. Jesus said, "I am the way, the truth, and the life. No one comes to the Father except through me" (John 14:6).

The Bible warns us about approaching the spiritual realm apart from Christ. New Age thought is basically religious, attempting to help people realize their greatest potential—the divine within.

The influence of New Age thinking should not be underestimated. New Agers are opinion-makers. Naisbitt says, "Ninety-five percent of the readers of the *New Age Journal* are college-educated, with average household incomes of $47,500. New Agers represent the most affluent, well-educated, successful segment of the baby boom."[4]

It is so easy for people to become involved with New Age thinking and organizations. The philosophy is so attractively packaged that it enlists the respectable leaders in business, science, medicine, and education, without their knowledge.

"Corporations spend an estimated $4 billion per year on New Age consultants. A *California Business* survey of 500 companies found that more than 50 percent had used 'consciousness-raising' techniques. Proctor & Gamble, TRW, Ford Motor Company, AT&T, IBM, and General Motors all have signed on New Age trainers."[5] If these were presented as openly occult, their views would be discarded, but cloaked in the respectability of self-help, productivity, and creativity, they are reaching a growing audience.

One writer-researcher said, "I once attended a day of lectures at a New Age retreat center near Baltimore, Maryland. One speaker summed his points up by explaining what was meant by the coming 'New Age' and then enthusiastically concluded with a statement that should chill Bible-believing Christians, '. . . it all started in Babylon, folks!'"[6]

He was right. The New Age is really the "doctrines of demons" wrapped in slick new packages.

Power-Hungry Woman

The scarlet woman who represents an apostate religious system is identified as "the great city that rules over the kings of the earth" (17:18). At the time when John wrote this, there could have been only one possible interpretation of that statement. John was talking about Rome. To his great astonishment, he sees a vast political and religious system centered at Rome and reaching out in all directions to grasp power. The "woman" sits upon the seven hills of Rome and is dressed in purple and scarlet.

The woman is in partnership with the political system of the Beast; the religious system she represents dominates the Antichrist. Power politics and power religion commit themselves to each other, but only for a time. Like many partnerships, one member of the team wants to buy out—or push out—the other.

Rich and Intoxicated Woman

This powerful prostitute has so much influence that her intoxicating wiles are practiced throughout the world. Revelation says that she influences "peoples, multitudes, nations and languages" (17:15). Mystery Babylon, the spiritual whore, establishes her base of operation in Rome, the logical place for a concentration of power. It was from Rome that the Caesars reached out to conquer the world of their day; from Rome, the papal authority has reached out in power to every corner of the earth. Romanism has misapplied the message of God's Word concerning His kingdom, since this church considers itself the only true church.

The scarlet woman represents an apostate religious system that will combine weak protestantism with catholicism, spiritualism, humanism, and the occult into one great satanic connection.

Partnership with the Beast

"I saw a woman sitting on a scarlet beast that was covered with blasphemous names and had seven heads and ten horns" (Revelation 17:3).

The woman and the Beast agree to combine their powers and take over the West. The seven heads and ten horns describe the political organization of the Beast, identified later in this chapter. This alliance will be so rich that all the oil barons of the Middle East will look like middle-class citizens.

Ms. Mystery Babylon will not be a soft-hearted madam with a "heart of gold," as the saloon-keepers in movie Westerns are portrayed, but "the woman was drunk with the blood of the saints, the blood of those who bore testimony to Jesus" (Revelation 17:6).

John could understand why pagan Rome would torture and kill believers, because he had seen this himself. But he was "greatly astonished" that religious Rome could be so cruel. As we look at the benevolent Roman church today, we find it hard to believe that it could ever be classified as "drunk with blood." If we study history, however, we will not have a difficult time understanding this imagery. *Halley's Bible Handbook* contains a detailed section on "The Inquisition," which gives us a view of Roman brutality:

> . . . the Inquisition was the main agency in the Papacy's effort to crush the Reformation. It is stated that in the 30 years

between 1540 and 1570, no fewer than 900,000 Protestants were put to death. Think of the monks and priests directing, with heartless cruelty and inhuman brutality, the work of torturing and burning alive innocent men and women; and doing it in the name of Christ, by the direct order of the "Vicar of Christ." The Inquisition is the most infamous thing in history. It was devised by the Popes, and used by them for 500 years to maintain their power.[7]

Yes, Rome has been drunk with the blood of the saints, and during the Tribulation those who have become believers will suffer intensely under the rule of the one-world church, Mystery Babylon.

Riding on the Back of the Beast

This is a case of female domination. The harlot system of religion dominates the Beast (Antichrist) and controls the leader of the Revived Roman Empire with tight reins for the first half of the Tribulation.

John was told by the angel who relayed this prophecy to him: "I will explain to you the mystery of the woman and of the beast she rides, which has the seven heads and ten horns. The beast, which you saw, once was, now is not, and will come up out of the Abyss and go to his destruction. The inhabitants of the earth whose names have not been written in the book of life from the creation of the world will be astonished when they see the beast, because he once was, now is not, and yet will come" (Revelation 17:7, 8).

When we first met this Beast, we were told that he came up out of the sea (Revelation 13), but now we are told that he comes up out of the Abyss. Is this the same person? He wears many hats, but when he first appears, he will be an ordinary human being. Remember that he will be killed and brought back to life again by satanic power. From then on, the Beast is more than a human being; he is a supernatural person, out of the bottomless pit. In his supernatural state, he will command the worship of the masses of people still on earth at that time.

This Beast is a real monster. He is described with seven heads and ten horns—an ugly image! The seven heads have two meanings: seven mountains and seven kings. The seven mountains are synonymous with the seven hills of Rome. The seven kings are explained this way:

"Five have fallen, one is, the other has not yet come; but when he does come, he must remain for a little while. The beast who once was, and now is not, is an eighth king. He belongs to the seven and is going to his destruction" (Revelation 17:9–11).

Dust off the ancient history and here's what we find: Five Roman kings or emperors had fallen when John was writing this prophecy—Julius Caesar, Tiberius, Caligula, Claudius, and Nero. The king who was reigning at this time (the "one is") was Domitian, that cruel despot who sent John to Patmos.

When John wrote this prophecy, one king was yet future. This seventh king, or kingdom, is the Revived Roman Empire, which will remain for three and a half years, headed by the Antichrist Roman ruler.

The ten horns are the ten-nation confederacy, which, I believe, has been formed in our time as the European Common Market. The nations that comprise this group will give the Beast his authority and power.

Harlot's Doom

Babylon the Great, the mother of prostitutes, symbolizes the religious system which will dominate the great one-world government with her seductive power.

The first half of the Tribulation, the Antichrist will tolerate this unholy alliance, until he decides the system is no longer useful to him. Perhaps he will be goaded into action by the false prophet, but his ambition is to set himself up as god and be worshiped. "The beast and the ten horns you saw will hate the prostitute. They will bring her to ruin and leave her naked; they will eat her flesh and burn her with fire" (Revelation 17:16).

As we picture the woman riding on the Beast and then being destroyed by him, a familiar limerick comes to mind:

> There was a young lady from Niger
> Who smiled as she rode on the Tiger.
> They came back from the ride with the lady inside
> And the smile on the face of the Tiger.

Here is a clear warning against the marriage of politics and religion. Whenever we see that liaison, history has shown that it ends in violent divorce.

Tale of Two Babylons, Continued

John is told about two stages in the fall of Babylon. An angel who "had great authority, and the earth was illuminated by his splendor" (Revelation 18:1), prophesied the destruction of another Babylon. The angel, who is so powerful that some scholars have thought that he is Jesus Christ Himself, pronounces judgment upon the city of Babylon.

"Fallen! Fallen is Babylon the Great!" (Revelation 18:2).

This shout is a sign of cataclysmic destruction. The repetition of the word is intended to describe two separate stages of the fall. The first refers to Babylon as a system of false worship (destroyed by the Antichrist), and the second to Babylon the city in which this spirit is embodied.[8]

Many believe this prophecy necessitates the actual rebuilding of Babylon on the banks of the Euphrates River. Since a few dusty ruins in the troubled country of Iraq are all that's left of that glittering city of ancient times, it is difficult to conceive that Babylon could be an important world center in the near future. However, Iraq has the oil-rich resources, including a pipeline which can carry some 1.6 billion barrels of oil a day to the Red Sea, that indicates this little country could show some strong economic power.[9] And there is no question but Saddan Hussein impacted the whole world with his invasion of Kuwait and threats to extend his power even further.

Others believe this Babylon will be a system of life and culture whose basic principle is alienation from God. It will be the wealthiest, most decadent metropolis the world has ever known. The destruction of this city by the hand of God will be done explosively—sixty minutes to ashes.

A German artist, Ludwig Meidner, has painted some violent landscapes depicting the end of the world. Meidner's work, which has achieved world-wide acclaim, includes one painting, "Apocalyptic Landscape"; it's an eerie preview of the last days. The purple emotions of this troubled artist expose the feelings of many people today who do not know Jesus Christ as their Savior. Meidner died in 1966, leaving a legacy of destruction on canvas, a holocaust without hope.

The Sins of Babylon

The city represented as Babylon will be the crime center of the world. "For her sins are piled up to heaven, and God has remembered her crimes" (Revelation 18:5). The sins of Babylon have piled one on another like bricks in the tower of Babel. Each stone is an indictment about its sick condition.

First, Babylon is judged because of her sin. Her character is despicable: she has become a "home for demons," a "haunt for every evil spirit, a haunt for every unclean and detestable bird." This is a repugnant description of the occultist system of the Beast, the foul spirits that will control the minds of men.

This image reminds me of the leering face of Richard Ramirez, the Night Stalker murderer, who gave a satanic sign when sentenced to death in a Los Angeles courtroom. Unrepentance is ugly in any form.

Babylon is judged because of her *influence*. She is the center of social, political, cultural, and commercial life on this globe. The trap set by this system will lead to its downfall. The Bible warns about rich oppressors:

> Now listen, you rich people, weep and wail because of the misery that is coming upon you. Your wealth has rotted, and moths have eaten your clothes. Your gold and silver are corroded. Their corrosion will testify against you and eat your flesh like fire. You have hoarded wealth in the last days. Look! The wages you failed to pay the workmen who mowed your fields are crying out against you. . . . You have lived on earth in luxury and self indulgence (James 5:1–5).

The robber barons of the end times will exceed all of the excesses of Cornelius Vanderbilt, once America's richest man who amassed more money in his personal coffers than was held in the U.S. Treasury.

Babylon is judged because of her *infidelity.* Living in iniquity and boasting of it, she is totally insensitive to the concept of a sovereign God.

Babylon will be judged because of her *inhumanity.* Along with merchant cargoes of luxury items, the ". . . bodies and souls of men" (18:13) will be bought and sold. Men and women will barter their bodies for some insignificant trifle. Human beings will be nothing more than commodities to own and sell. This world system championed by the beast will dehumanize mankind, as any system without God will do.

Mourning of the Damned

All the luxury and arrogant splendor of this city will be gone in one hour. "The merchants who sold these things and gained with wealth from her will stand far off, terrified at her torment. They will weep and mourn and cry out" (18:15).

The sea captains will watch the smoke of her burning. They will weep over the loss of their lucrative shipping trade. The city will lose its music, the workmen their jobs. Darkness will envelop the streets once brilliant with lights, theater marquees, and neon enticements. In this city where the best-dressed of all the world paraded their designer fashions, the costly garments will be gone. One of the saddest statements is that "the voice of bridegroom and bride will never be heard in you again" (18:23). The rejoicings of a wedding, which stands for one of the highest of all human joys, will be silenced.

John sees a mighty angel hurl a boulder the size of a large millstone into the sea as a symbol of the violent destruction of Babylon (18:21). When the Lord was on the earth, He said it was better for man to have a millstone hung around his neck and be drowned in the depth of the sea than offend one of God's little ones. "Offend" is too weak a word to describe what this great godless power, filled with the blood of saints and prophets, will do. Mystery Babylon will be thrown into the abyss of judgment.

Rejoicing in a Book of Tears

"Rejoice, saints and apostles and prophets! God has judged her for the way she treated you" (18:20).

The saints are in heaven and they are worshiping, honoring, and praising God in His glory. But now the saints are called to look down upon the world they left. They see that the vile Babylon of godless men has come to final doom and this world system will never rise again. This is cause for celebration.

Escape from Babylon

In the midst of the description of the fall of Babylon, John hears a voice from heaven that says:

"Come out of her, my people, so that you will not share in her sins, so that you will not receive any of her plagues; for her sins are piled up to heaven, and God has remembered her crimes" (18:4).

God's people will not be in Babylon at the time of its destruction, but we can become involved in the sins of Babylon in our present life on earth. Paul wrote these instructions to the people of Corinth: "Do not be yoked together with unbelievers. For what do righteousness and wickedness have in common? Or what fellowship can light have with darkness?" (2 Corinthians 6:14).

Fleeing from Babylon is the route to take from the judgments of Babylon. In today's self-centered, materialistic world, it's not an easy journey, but the destination is worth the trip.

Part IV

THE WORLD FOREVER:
RECLAIMED BY GOD

16

IT IS DONE!

The Apocalypse is so full of suffering and destruction . . . why does a loving God allow all this? Doesn't love mean compassion, caring for someone more than he cares for you? Aren't we supposed to love our enemies? These questions plague the person who does not understand the attributes of our Creator God.

In this twentieth century, men have replaced God's holiness with a God of sweetness and light. How often do we hear of God's judgment? It is not a popular subject and doesn't provide a catchy sermon title for the church bulletin. The crowds come to have their ears tickled, not their consciences rattled.

In the majestic song of Moses, we hear, "Who among the gods is like you, O Lord? Who is like you—majestic in holiness, awesome in glory, working wonders?" (Exodus 15:11).

In our generation we have lost sight of the holiness of God as the focus of His nature. God has been called "The Man Upstairs," as if He sits in the clouds, pulling the strings of earthly puppets. Or He is the "good Lord," which is a pablum version of His majesty.

When we comprehend God's holy attributes, we will begin to see the necessity of the judgments during the Tribulation.

J. Vernon McGee describes man's dilemma with his inimitable directness: "After almost a century of insipid preaching from America's pulpits, the average man believes that God is all sweetness and light and would not discipline or punish anyone. Well, this Book of Revelation tells a different story!"[1]

Six Angel-Messengers

John must have rubbed his old eyes many times during the visions he was given on Patmos. In the fourteenth chapter of Revelation he tells us about some advance agents who make announcements that tie together the rest of the book.

In Greek drama, battles and important events were not always enacted on the stage because they would have been too complicated for a small cast of actors to handle. Instead, they were announced by messengers. This is the role of these six angels. We are not expected to understand their announcements chronologically.

The first angel announces the gospel, but not as we know it in this present age. There is no altar call or invitation to salvation. It is a gospel that emphasizes the creative work of God.

Dr. Henry Morris wrote: "If Christ is not the Creator, He can hardly be the Savior or the coming King. These men of the last days must first be called back to believe in a true creation and therefore a real Creator God before they can ever be constrained to come to Him as Savior."[2]

In our day, when the battle between the creationists and the evolutionists rages in our educational system, it should be noted that the angel stresses creation, whereas the world's inhabitants have been indoctrinated with the godless philosophy of evolution.

This angel carried the "eternal gospel to proclaim to those who live on the earth" (14:6). This is the only place in the Bible where that exact statement is made. How appropriate

it is during these dark ages when men will be blindly worshiping the Beast and his image, that one last attempt is made to
call men back to the fear of the living God and to worship
Him.

The second angel announces the fall of Babylon that was
described in the previous chapter. Of course, followers of Satan
will not listen to their coming destruction even if angels stand
in front of them waving large red flags.

The third angel announces the options of the earthdwellers: worship the Beast and be damned by God or worship
God and be damned by the Beast. There's no in-between. Compromise has never been a part of God's word, and this messenger will announce that the torment for those who worship the
Beast will last forever, but the torment for those who refuse
the mark will only last for a while and then there will be glory
forever and ever.

There are thousands of saints in the Tribulation period,
and they will wonder how they will receive their future reward.
They were too late for the Rapture. But God has a special blessing for them. "They will rest from their labor, for their deeds
will follow them" (Revelation 14:13).

Many people think that heaven will be a place of boredom
and idle inactivity. But when the Lord says "rest," He means
refreshment. In heaven we will be involved in serving, but without the tiredness and fatigue that often accompanies our work
on earth. We will not need vitamin tablets or caffeine.

Saturday Evening of the Age

We are about to see through John's eyes the last activity
on the earth as we know it. The final set of seven judgments are
released before the glorious event of the second coming of
Jesus Christ.

A brief review indicates that the scroll has reached the
end. As it unrolled, we saw seven seal judgments (Revelation 5,
6, and 8), then the seven trumpet judgments (Revelation 8, 9,

and 11). Now we will see the seven bowl judgments poured out during the reign of the Beast.

Seven angels are the messengers who receive direct orders from God Himself, as He speaks in a loud voice from the inner temple. God's patience throughout the centuries comes to a final end. He tells the seven angels, "Go, pour out the seven bowls of God's wrath on the earth" (Revelation 16:1).

The First Bowl Judgment: Loathsome Sores

This will not be a pretty sight. When the first angel is commanded to pour out his bowl, ". . . ugly and painful sores broke out on the people who had the mark of the beast" (Revelation 16:2).

These sores are just the beginning of the torments they will know for eternity. Loathsome skin diseases are significant because they are outward signs of inward corruption. Jesus described those who looked good on the outside, but were rotten to the core, when He spoke to the self-righteous leaders of His day:

"Woe to you, teachers of the law and Pharisees, you hypocrites! You are like whitewashed tombs, which look beautiful on the outside but on the inside are full of dead men's bones and everything unclean" (Matthew 23:27).

The curse of the sores was prophesied by Moses when the people of Israel refused to follow the law, and worshiped strange gods. Here is what Moses said:

"The Lord will afflict you with the boils of Egypt and with tumors, festering sores and the itch, from which you cannot be cured. . . . The Lord will afflict your knees and legs with painful boils that cannot be cured, spreading from the soles of your feet to the top of your head" (Deuteronomy 28:27, 35).

Just reading that makes my skin crawl. As far as we know, this prophecy was never totally completed in Israel's history. The people on earth who have followed the Antichrist will experience the painful fulfillment of this curse.

The Second and Third Bowls: Water Turned to Blood

"The second angel poured out his bowl on the sea, and it turned into blood like that of a dead man, and every living thing in the sea died. The third angel poured out his bowl on the rivers and springs of water, and they became blood" (Revelation 16:3, 4).

I don't believe it is a coincidence that the second seal (the red horse of war), the second trumpet (a third of the sea turned into blood), and the second bowl, all have to do with blood.

Imagine all the salt-water fish and all the fresh-water fish dying. The stench throughout the land would be oppressive. Moreover, what will people drink? The cans of soft drinks and the bottles of juices cannot last forever.

The reason for these judgments is that the blood of saints and prophets was shed. The altar will be the shelter of the martyrs in Revelation (chapter six) and now their cry for revenge is being answered.

Everyone who has criticized the Lord for judgment is silenced as a result of the martyrs saying "Yes, Lord God Almighty, true and just are your judgments" (16:7).

The prophet Habakkuk summed it up: "The Lord is in his holy temple; let all the earth be silent before him" (2:20).

The Fourth Bowl: Intense Heat

The fourth angel will give the sun power to scorch people with fire. People will be seared by the intense heat, and many will die with curses on their burning tongues.

All God would have to do to make this judgment happen is remove one or two ozone layers of the atmosphere. A few years ago, no one seemed too bothered about changes in the climate. Now, weather is not just a conversation opener, but a cause for alarm. Scientists see the warming of the earth as an increasing threat to life-support systems. The Worldwatch Institute Report said, "The ozone layer in the upper atmosphere that protects us from ultraviolet radion is thinning. The very temperature of the earth appears to be rising, posing a threat of unknown dimensions to virtually all the life-support systems on which humanity depends."[3]

It doesn't matter what form God uses to cause this fiery plague, it will happen. Hundreds of years before Christ, the prophet Malachi wrote: "'Surely the day is coming; it will burn like a furnace. All the arrogant and every evildoer will be stubble, and that day that is coming will set them on fire,' says the Lord Almighty" (4:1).

The Fifth Bowl: Blackness in Satan's Kingdom

God will center His judgment upon the place of Satan himself. This plague will bring darkness, and as people gnaw their tongues with pain from the sores and the heat, they will continue to curse God and refuse to repent.

Darkness is a familiar theme in the Word of God. Many of the prophets spoke of coming darkness (Isaiah 60:2; Joel 2:2), and Jesus said during the Tribulation, ". . . the sun will be darkened, and the moon will not give its light" (Mark 13:24).

My imagination is stretched to comprehend the horror and agony of these judgments. I can understand how Bible readers would want to skip some of these chapters and turn to a soothing Psalm or a teaching parable. But every portion of God's Word is "useful for teaching, rebuking, correcting and training in righteousness" (2 Timothy 3:16).

The Sixth Bowl: Euphrates Dries Up

We never hear of anyone taking a cruise on the Euphrates. In fact, if you asked a dozen people where the river is, perhaps one or two might know its general location. Why would it be so important that the sixth angel was commanded to dry it up?

This judgment is more than a plague, it is a prelude to

the gathering of the troops for Armageddon. Listen to the approaching cadence of an immense oriental army: "The sixth angel poured out his bowl on the great river Euphrates, and its water was dried up to prepare the way for the kings from the east" (16:12).

John has told us about four vicious angels who were kept in bondage by God at the Euphrates River, and upon their release an incredible army of "200 million" troops swarm into the Middle East.

The Euphrates is the largest river in western Asia and from time immemorial has been a formidable boundary between the peoples east of it and those on the west. History frequently refers to the hindrance the Euphrates has been to military movements, but in these last days the 1,800 miles of its winding depths will be the pavement for the march to the final battlefield.

The sixth angel has some more judgments in his bowl, and these are "three evil spirits that looked like frogs; they came out of the mouth of the dragon, out of the mouth of the beast and out of the mouth of the prophet. They are spirits of demons performing miraculous signs, and they go out to the kings of the whole world, to gather them for the battle on the great day of God Almighty" (16:13, 14).

Here's the unholy trinity again: Satan, Antichrist, and the false prophet. They get together in their war room to make an attempt to get the nations of the world to march against Israel and defeat God's purposes on earth.

For some time I puzzled how all the earth's leaders would be provoked to fight against the armies of the Lord. The nation of Israel is such a tiny piece of real estate in the vast expanses of this world—on some maps it takes a magnifying glass to find it! Then I realized that those "frogs," with their incessant croaking, would creep out of dark shadows and stir up noisy demonstrations until all the heads of nations and kings of countries would be infused with hatred for the final crushing of God and all His powers.

One commentator called them the "grand army of the Devil's worshippers."

Warning before the Last Bowl Is Poured

Before God allows the last bowl to be poured out upon the earth, there is one more warning. He makes another statement about His coming in judgment and the opportunity to be prepared: "Behold, I come like a thief!" (16:15).

It's important to realize that Christ will never come as a thief to the church. "But you, brothers, are not in darkness so that this day should surprise you like a thief" (1 Thessalonians 4:5). Christians are looking for the glorious appearing of our Lord, anticipating His return for us.

At the end of the Great Tribulation, the Lord will come as an unwelcome intruder, and the whole earth will mourn because of Him.

The Final Bowl of Judgment

"The seventh angel poured out his bowl into the air, and out of the temple came a loud voice from the throne, saying, 'It is done!'" (16:17).

As the last bowl of judgment is tipped, it is followed by thunders, lightnings, the worst earthquake ever experienced, and hailstones weighing about one hundred pounds. This is the final destruction of every religious, political, and educational institution that man has built apart from God. It is the collapse of all men's hopes and dreams for earthly power. God says, "It is done." Once before we heard these words from the cross, as God finished the judgment upon men's sins. Now these words are heard again as the judgment upon the earth is complete.

The kings of the earth will gather in a place called Armageddon. How many times do we hear that location mentioned in our own experience, and yet this is the only place where that word is found in all the Bible! The word means

"Mount of Megiddo," and the valley of Megiddo is located about fifteen miles southeast of modern Haifa.

It is awesome to stand on a steep path overlooking this fertile valley and realize that some day the carnage there will be worse than any battle fought throughout the ages.

A gruesome description of this devastation is given in Revelation 14:20, when we are told that blood will flow as high as horse's bridles for a distance of 200 miles. The only valley of that length in Israel is the Jordan River valley, which goes from the Sea of Galilee through the Dead Sea and down to the Gulf of Eliat. That valley will have a red river of blood running through it.

Identity of All the King's Men

Armageddon will not be a one-day battle; it will be a continual campaign from the time the Lord releases the deadly war machine of the red horse. Wars will rage on earth until the final battle occurs in the valley of decision.

John has not told us who the "kings of the whole earth" will be, but other prophets have written their I.D.'s. One of the kings of the earth will be the King of the South, described in Psalm 83:1-8 and in Daniel 11:20. This king, whom Bible scholars identify as Egypt and its confederates from Arab and African nations, will attack the Israeli false prophet (see the Malicious Masquerade in chapter 15). The false prophet, who is the Antichrist's co-conspirator, will probably be a Jew with his base of operation in Jerusalem.

When Israel is invaded by armies of the *King of the South* in a vicious attempt to destroy it, another implacable enemy of Israel, the *King of the North,* will launch an all-out invasion. Most students of prophecy today believe that this northern monarch could be none other than Russia and its allies (see Daniel 11:40-45; Ezekiel 38:14-17; Joel 2:1-10, 20).

We believe that the opening of the second seal (Revelation 6:3, 4) signals the beginning of these invasions. At that time the rider on a red horse takes the false peace, promised by the Antichrist, from the world. According to the prophet Daniel, the King of the South and the King of the North will join forces in their attack on Israel. However, this alliance will be short-lived, as Russia continues on to Egypt and takes control of the southern kingdom, evidently double-crossing the Arabs and their allies (see Daniel 11:40–43).

The King of the North will have established headquarters in Egypt or Africa, but will not have much time to revel in his triumph because messengers are telling him about threats from the east and north. From the east he hears about a great army of millions beginning to mobilize. North of Egypt is Israel, where the Roman Antichrist, who heads the ten nations of the Revived Roman Empire, is preparing his military machine.

The King of the North will be completely annihilated in Israel. The prophet Ezekiel said all the troops of the northern commander would fall and their bodies would be food for birds and wild animals (Ezekiel 39:4–6).

The invasion of Israel by the King of the North, with all its devastation, is only a preview of the Great War. No nation will escape the global catastrophe to come.

The armies of the King of the East prepare to attack the Antichrist, who will be in Israel at that time. This Oriental horde will cross the dried-up Euphrates to begin its death march.

Today's Front Page

Who can we believe? The global media brings us reassuring pictures of amiable summit meetings and we settle in our chairs, lulled once more into false security. The next day another tyrant threatens the unsteady peace, sky-rocketing the world's blood pressure once again as the news pundits maneuver our minds with their reports. Only God's Word is trustworthy.

The 1960s and 1970s saw people aroused to action by prophecy. The 1980s have seen people slip into disinterest and apathy. We must not allow the present world events to distract us from proclaiming the truth of things to come. The apostle Paul says he learned to be content in whatever his circumstances, but he never said to be complacent!

The Battle of Armageddon

Armageddon will be different from any war man has experienced in history. Supernatural events that our finite minds cannot comprehend will be taking place.

Jerusalem, the prized city of the world which has been conquered and rebuilt throughout the centuries, is nearly one hundred miles from the combat zone. But this Holy City will not be spared from the conflict. The prophet Zechariah said, "I will gather all the nations to Jerusalem to fight against it; the city will be captured, the houses ransacked, and the women raped. Half of the city will go into exile, but the rest of the people will not be taken from the city" (14:2).

For centuries Jerusalem, the Holy City, has seen invasions, destruction, and rapings. Now it will see one last catastrophe. As the battle rages, every city of the nations will be leveled by a giant earthquake or a great shaking of the earth, which could be a nuclear exchange when the red buttons are pushed in every capitol.

The seventh angel has poured out his bowl (Revelation 16:17–21) and all the great cities are going to fall under judgment at that time. There will be no doubt that the end has come.

Incredible Miracle in Israel

However, we have been told by God's prophets of a great spiritual awakening that will take place in this battered city and land in the time of Armageddon. In the time of Moses, God delivered Israel out of Egypt in a miraculous way. In the time of Armageddon, He will do the same for His people. The Jews will experience a mass conversion. It will be the greatest Jews-for-Jesus rally in all history.

The prophet Zechariah said: "On that day the Lord will shield those who live in Jerusalem, so that the feeblest among them will be like David, and the house of David will be like God, like the angel of the Lord going before them. On that day I will set out to destroy all the nations that attack Jerusalem" (12:8, 9).

"And so all Israel will be saved" (Romans 11:26).

How exciting it is to know that one day those who have rejected their Messiah will accept Him—at last! The Wailing Wall, where devout Jews pray, may be smashed to dust, but the Savior they ignored will then be embraced.

When He prophesied the destruction of Jerusalem, Jesus told the Jews that they would not see Him again until they welcomed Him as the blessed one who comes in the name of the Lord (Matthew 23:37–39).

The Israelis have been tough in the Six-Day War and the Yom Kippur War, but in those final days, they will fight with more strength than ever before. They will lead His people in battle and all the nations that seek to destroy Israel will be annihilated (see Zechariah 12:9 and 14:3–4).

Wheat and Grape Harvests

One of the common references for judgment in the Old Testament is the picture of a harvest. In the days preceding His coming, Jesus will reap the harvest, gathering in the wheat and separating it from the tares (Revelation 14:14–16). To understand this harvest, let's look at what Matthew said:

". . . The one who sowed the good seed is the Son of Man. The field is the world, and the good seed stands for the sons of the kingdom. The weeds are the sons of the evil one, and the enemy who sows them is the devil. The harvest is the end of the age, and the harvesters are angels" (13:37).

What we may not have understood in Matthew, we see in Revelation. How exciting it is to see the complete agreement of prophecy throughout the Bible!

Jesus does not actually do the dividing Himself, but carefully supervises the separation of the wheat and tares so that not one believer is judged with unbelievers. This separation work done by angels happens just before His triumphant return to earth.

Finally, John sees another angel coming from the Temple of heaven, gathering all the clusters of grapes into "the great winepress of God's wrath." It is now that we see the true "Grapes of Wrath" being trampled in the winepress: "And blood flowed out of the press, rising as high as the horses' bridles for a distance of 1,600 stadia" [the length of Israel from north to south] (Revelation 14:20).

The armies of all nations will be gathered in Israel, particularly around Jerusalem—200 million Orientals, along with troops from the Revived Roman Empire, headed by the Antichrist. The Beast will be joined by the false prophet and all the world military leaders as Goliath-like forces descend upon the Holy Land with every piece of sophisticated weaponry man has designed. The Normandy landing of the Allied forces in World War II was a skirmish compared to this last battle.

Then an astounding, shocking, amazing, predictable thing will occur. "Then the Lord will go out and fight against those nations, as he fights in the day of battle. *On that day* his feet will stand on the Mount of Olives, east of Jerusalem, and the Mount of Olives will be split in two from east to west, forming a great valley" (Zechariah 14:3, 4).

He will return to the blessed place where He ascended to heaven, His beloved Mount of Olives, adjacent to the Temple site. The armies of the world who attack Jerusalem may never know what hit them. The prophet Zechariah said: "This is the plague with which the Lord will strike all the nations that fought against Jerusalem: Their flesh will rot while they are still standing on their feet, their eyes will rot in their sockets, and their tongues will rot in their mouths" (14:12).

On that day, Jesus Christ will return, and we shall return with Him, if we have accepted Him as our Savior during our earthly life. This is the most important travel reservation we could ever make.

17

THE SECOND COMING

The alarm goes off and you stumble out of bed at the beginning of a new day. You switch on the radio for the morning news, and instead of the latest war, the most recent major catastrophe, or the stock market report, the announcer reports that Jesus Christ will return tonight at seven.

Of course, that will never happen, for Christ Himself said that no one knows the day or hour of His return. But what if we did know that today would be our last day on earth? How would we react? Would we hurry to say "I'm sorry" to someone we had hurt? Would we rush to our neighbors, or co-workers, or someone in our own family and say, "I've got something extremely important to tell you—Jesus is coming tonight. Do you know Him as your personal Savior?"

A poet said:

> Some day that dawns will make all time as past,
> Then may we keep our lamps all trimmed and bright,
> Oh, may we live each day as if it were the last,
> And ready be if Christ should come tonight.

It's one thing to talk about, preach about, and read about the second coming of Christ, and another to believe it. All history will culminate in this event, and yet it has been a neglected subject in this present age. On Sunday we sing "Jesus Is Coming Again," but on Monday morning it is forgotten.

As I write this book, I do not know if it will ever be read. He may return before it is finished. However, right now it is a thrill to tell about a dramatic change that will happen at the end of the Great Tribulation.

All the horrors, that John and other prophets have recorded, are past. Babylon, the capitol of the Beast and the center of all false religion, greed, and evil works, has been destroyed. The darkness will turn to light. The sober will give way to song. And look who's singing. . . .

Celebration in Heaven

"After this, I heard what sounded like the roar of a great multitude in heaven shouting: 'Hallelujah! Salvation and glory and power belong to our God, for true and just are his judgments. He has condemned the great prostitute who corrupted the earth by her adulteries. He has avenged on her the blood of his servants'" (Revelation 19:1, 2).

Five shouts of "Praise the Lord" resound throughout heaven as there is a great preparation for Jesus' return. The angels, the Old Testament saints, the church saints, and the Tribulation saints will raise their voices in a choir which will reverberate louder than thunder. I've heard great choirs before, but I'm really looking forward to being in this one.

What a Hallelujah chorus it will be!

Some can't understand how people in heaven can rejoice when sinners are condemned. We have seen how God has vindicated Himself upon the false system of worship and the whole economic system of the Beast. Until this time, the redeemed have been delivered from the power and penalty of sin, but now they will be delivered from the very *presence* of sin. The psalmist wrote: "But may sinners vanish from the earth and the wicked be no more. Praise the Lord, O my soul. Praise the Lord" (Psalm 104:35).

Old John's eyes must have filled with happy tears as he saw the four and twenty elders and the four beasts (see Revelation 4), joining in this mighty chorus and crying out, "Amen, Hallelujah!"

No matter what race or tongue, there is a universal language among Christians.

The story is told of two men who met on board a luxury liner. One was a missionary heading for the foreign field, and the other was a young national believer. Both felt out of place on board that ship, for gambling and drinking were the predominant pastimes. They were pacing the deck one night, carrying their Bibles. When they met, they tried to exchange greetings, but there was a language barrier. Then the young national had a great idea. "Hallelujah," he said. The missionary smiled and said, "Amen." They had a common tongue.

The Ceremony in Heaven

When John heard these heavenly voices, he recorded chapter nineteen of Revelation, which is the bridge between the Great Tribulation and the Millennium or the kingdom of Our Lord.

The great hallelujah/amen chorus is a prelude to the most magnificent wedding festivities of the ages:

> Let us rejoice and be glad and give him glory! For the wedding of the Lamb has come, and his bride has made herself ready. Fine linen, bright and clean, was given her to wear. Then the angel said to me, "Write: 'Blessed are those who are invited to the wedding supper of the Lamb!'" And he added, "These are the true words of God" (Revelation 19:7–9).

We are invited to see (and participate in) two loving ceremonies which will usher in that long-awaited event—the second coming of Christ.

In the Bible the church is the bride of Jesus Christ. The apostle Paul wrote: "For this reason a man will leave his father and mother and will be united to his wife, and the two will become one flesh. This is a profound mystery—but I am talking about Christ and the church" (Ephesians 5:31, 32).

Old Oriental marriage customs will help us understand these ceremonies: the wedding of the Lamb and the wedding supper of the Lamb.

In the first century, and for centuries to follow, there were usually three steps to follow from the time of betrothal of a young couple until the final marriage union. First, the parents of the bride and the bridegroom negotiated a marriage contract, usually when the couple was very young. They were legally married, although there was no sexual contact for years. This betrothal was not like the engagement period today; it was much more binding.

The second step in this marriage took place when the bridegroom, accompanied by some friends, went to the bride's house to take her back to his own home.

Finally, the bridal procession would be followed by the marriage feast, which would last for many days.

In the same manner, the believer in Jesus Christ has already entered into the legal contract of marriage to Christ at the time of his conversion. The bride (the church) is waiting eagerly for the time when the Bridegroom will come and take her back to the prepared mansion where the marriage of the Lamb will take place. This is the second step in the marriage ceremony.

Today's weddings center on the bride. There are bridal showers and bridal shops, fashion shows for the bride, and special luncheons for her bridesmaids. But the groom wears a rented suit. At the Oriental marriage, the groom is the Very Important Person. So it will be in the marriage of the Lamb; the bride must take second place to the blessed Lamb of Calvary.

The Church Is the Bride; Christ Is the Bridegroom

When Christ returns at the Rapture, He takes his beloved bride, the Church, to be with Him in the beautiful home He has prepared for her. The bride lays her dowry of crowns at His feet. What a beautiful picture of love and adoration we find in Revelation 19:7, 8: "'His bride has made herself ready. Fine linen, bright and clean, was given her to wear.' (Fine linen stands for the righteous acts of the saints.)"

The wedding gown will be made by the master Designer, and it symbolizes the righteous deeds done by the bride on earth through the power of the Holy Spirit. Believers will stand before Christ and have their works tested before they are fit to be presented to Him as His bride. The lavishness or the drabness of that wedding gown (the fine linen) will be determined by a report on the deeds performed on earth in the Spirit, not in the flesh. How we use the gifts God gave us on earth will decide the way we are presented to the Bridegroom when He comes. Will we be dressed shabbily or lavishly?

Why is it the wedding of the Lamb? "Why not under one of the 700 or more titles ascribed to Him in the Scriptures? . . . Why? Because it was the Lamb you fell in love with. You didn't fall in love with a Creator, or a King, or a Lord. Think back and you will recall that those were the very things that drove you from Him. But it was different when you came to see Him as the Savior who shed His blood for you."[1]

The wedding of the Lamb takes place in heaven, after the judgment seat of Christ, but the wedding supper of the Lamb takes place on earth, after the second coming.

The Wedding Supper

In Bible times, the length of the wedding supper depended upon the wealth of the one hosting the feast. Since our Father owns it all, this wedding supper will be the longest in history— it will last a thousand years!

Several places in the New Testament there are references to the fact that this event is to take place on earth, and that it definitely involves Israel (see Matthew 22:1–14, Luke 14:16–25, and Matthew 25:1–13, where Israel is waiting for the return of the bridegroom and the bride and the wedding feast is located on earth).

Who will be present at this grand occasion? The center of attraction will be Jesus Christ the Bridegroom. No marriage supper is complete without the bride, the Church. However, there are other invited guests. I believe Israel (miraculously converted during the Tribulation) will be present, along with the saints who survive the Tribulation and the resurrected Old Testament saints (Daniel 12:2). Some of these "guests" will go into the thousand-year kingdom in their mortal bodies, while all those who return to earth with the Bridegroom (meaning the Church and resurrected Old Testament saints) will have their immortal bodies.

Imagine spending a thousand years on a honeymoon with the Lord Jesus Christ. But remember—this is only the beginning.

The Person of Prophecy

John heard the great hallelujahs and amens sung by the heavenly choirs, and an angel (how God uses these heavenly messengers!) announced the wedding supper. John was so overcome that he fell down to worship the angel.

This angel was powerful, for he was the one whom Revelation 18:1 told us had great authority and splendor. I think if I saw an angel like that I'd fall on my knees, too.

But the angel told John not to worship him, because he was just another servant of Jesus. He said, "Worship God! For the testimony of Jesus is the spirit of prophecy."

Prophecy is not a fortune teller, an astrologist, or a good-guesser. Prophecy is a Person.

If this mighty angel refused to be worshiped, how does

any created being have the audacity to command worship? Most religions of the world have a person who is adulated like a god. These men (and women) are false Christs and someday their kingdoms will crumble. They may flourish and entice converts for a time, but they have no future without repentance and acceptance of Jesus as Savior.

Behold a White Horse!

I cannot describe the overwhelming event that the hallelujah/amen chorus proclaimed. For the second time John saw heaven open. The first time, Jesus Christ caught up the saints with Him in the Rapture. This time, He returns with the saints in the Second Advent.

He will come on a white stallion, which to the ancient world represented a figure of conquest. John's description is so stirring that just reading it sends chills down my spine.

"I saw heaven standing open and there before me was a white horse, whose rider is called Faithful and True. With justice he judges and makes war. His eyes are like blazing fire, and on his head are many crowns. He has a name written on him that no one knows but he himself. He is dressed in a robe dipped in blood, and his name is the Word of God" (Revelation 19:11).

This is an event everyone can see. Some have said that we won't need technology, that Christ is capable of staging His return without science. This is true. However, it is even more plausible to us with the development of satellite capabilities. In the first century believers could not comprehend what to us is possible.

From Old Testament prophets to present-day believers, millions of saints have longed for the moment they could see Jesus return as King of kings and Lord of lords to establish His kingdom of peace and justice on this embattled planet. How exciting it is to know that we will be a part of the great army that returns with Him.

It is amazing to me that many teachers and pastors in Christian leadership doubt that Christ will return in person. Without belief in the Second Coming, we might as well rip out many passages in our Bible. In the Old Testament, the prophet Zechariah predicted (500 years before Christ was born) that His feet would stand on the Mount of Olives, which a great earthquake would cause to split in two (14:4). Christ will return to the very place from which He left! In the New Testament, Christ tells His disciples about His return, and describes the events which will precede it (Matthew 24:27–31).

When Jesus returns it will be to execute judgment on those who have rejected Him throughout the ages. At His first coming He was the Lamb who came to take away the sins of the world, but at His second coming He is "Faithful and True" in carrying out every promise He ever made. His blazing eyes will pierce the hearts of those who denied Him, and His clothing will be stained with the blood of His enemies.

The crowns He wears will be the many titles He has been given. In our finite minds we cannot comprehend the infinite names of Jesus. When we sing, "All hail the power of Jesus' name! Let angels prostrate fall; Bring forth the royal diadem, And crown Him Lord of all," we are proclaiming His coming again.

Armies Dressed in White

When we return with Him we will have immaculate white uniforms and be mounted on prancing white horses. I have often wondered how we could be part of an army that would go into the fracas in Armageddon, and not have clothing stained in blood. Then I realized that when the Lord speaks, the battle is over. No one will lift a finger against us.

"Out of his mouth comes a sharp sword with which to strike down the nations" (Revelation 19:15), and all of His enemies will be destroyed. The Tribulation believers who are still living at that time will be delivered from any further torment.

Vultures on the Last Battlefield

This is not a scene I enjoy writing about. It has been thrilling to know that we will be blessed with an invitation to the wedding supper of the Lamb, but it is depressing to realize that millions of unrepentant, hardened followers of the Antichrist and the False Prophet will be present for a brief time at what is called "the great supper of God."

Here is the gruesome scene of Armageddon's finale:

"And I saw an angel standing in the sun, who cried in a loud voice to all the birds flying in midair, 'Come, gather together for the great supper of God, so that you may eat the flesh of kings, generals, and mighty men, of horses and their riders, and the flesh of all people, free and slave, small and great'" (Revelation 19:17).

I'm glad that I have a confirmed reservation at the wedding supper of the Lamb, for at the other supper, instead of eating the food, the participants will *be* the food.

The Beast, the False Prophet, and All the King's Men

The Roman Antichrist and the False Prophet, who have brainwashed unbelievers to follow them, will be judged immediately by the Lord Jesus Christ. Their acts of ultimate evil will be so monstrous that they will be thrown alive into the "fiery lake of burning sulfur" (Revelation 19:20).

Judgment upon this devilish duo will be immediate. They will be cast into the place which will be described in the next chapter as the "second death." They will not be present at the Great White Throne Judgment, which will be held at the end of the thousand-year reign of the Kingdom of God on earth.

The Beast and the False Prophet are the first inhabitants of the eternal hell.

Who Believes in Hell Today?

If we went on a national television talk show and told our views on the reality of hell, we would not be popular. Nor would we be believed. Hell is not "in" today. Church historian Martin Marty said, "Hell disappeared. And no one noticed."[2]

"'Even conservative evangelicals are losing their taste for fire and brimstone' . . . says University of Virginia sociologist James Hunter, author of two books on contemporary evangelicalism. 'Many evangelicals have a difficult time conceiving of people, especially virtuous nonbelievers, going to hell.'"[3]

We have heard it said that if hell has disappeared from the current theological scene, can heaven be far behind?

"Within some liberal religious circles it already has slipped from polite conversation. 'There's not much hell and not much heaven either,' observes United Church of Christ theologian Max Stackhouse, a professor at Andover-Newton Theological School. 'The prevailing opinion is that when you die you're dead but God still cares.'"[4]

Jesus possessed the most compassionate heart that ever beat in a man, and yet He spoke of hell, He warned of hell, He described hell. However, most preachers today may extol the glories of heaven, but repress the horrors of hell.

I believe the Bible. It tells us that heaven and hell are real. It also tells us that Jesus is coming again. How should we respond? Some will retain the status quo, unaffected in thought or deed by the knowledge of this awesome event. Others will have the fire of a first love rekindled in their hearts.

What is your response?

Because He Is Coming Again —

1. *We should refrain from judging others.* When Christ returns, "He will bring to light what is hidden in darkness and will expose the motives of men's hearts" (1 Corinthians 4:5).

2. *We should remember the Lord's table.* "For whenever you eat this bread and drink this cup, you proclaim the Lord's death until he comes" (1 Corinthians 11:26).

3. *We can relate to one another in love.* "May the Lord make your love increase and overflow for each other and for everyone else, just as ours does for you. May he give you inner strength that you may be blameless and holy in the presence of our God and Father when our Lord Jesus comes with all his holy ones" (1 Thessalonians 3:12, 13).

4. *We can restore the bereaved.* "For the Lord himself will come down from heaven, with a loud command, with the voice of the archangel and with the trumpet call of God, and the dead in Christ will rise first" (1 Thessalonians 4:16).

5. *We may recommit ourselves to ministry.* "In the presence of God and of Christ Jesus, who will judge the living and the dead, and in view of his appearing and his kingdom, I give you this charge: Preach the Word; be prepared in season and out of season; correct, rebuke and encourage—with great patience and careful instruction" (2 Timothy 4:1, 2).

6. *We should refuse to neglect church.* "Let us not give up meeting together, as some are in the habit of doing, but let us encourage one another—and all the more as you see the Day approaching" (Hebrews 10:25).

7. *We should remain steadfast.* "You too, be patient and stand firm, because the Lord's coming is near" (James 5:8).

8. *We should reach the lost for Jesus Christ.* ". . . snatch others from the fire and save them" (Jude 21:23).

Prophecy is not simply a subject listing in an encyclopedia, placed there to satisfy an intellectual appetite. Revelation was not written to be hidden in the recesses of Christian curiosity.

Believing biblical prophecy should motivate us to depopulate hell. If the task seems too overwhelming, consider one small step: pray for one person to hear the gospel before it's too late. This one thing we can do.

18

THE THOUSAND YEARS

Peace may be found in two places: a man's heart and the dictionary. If bumper stickers are indicators of current thought, the one that says "PEACE NOW" is a desire which will have to be postponed for a few years.

From time immemorial man has looked for peace. He has joined peace movements, marched for peace, given prizes for peace, and gone to war for peace. When I hear of someone being arrested for disturbing the peace, I wonder where he found any.

Although people long for it, pray for it, fight and die for it, the Golden Age never seems to come. Some day, however, during the thousand-year kingdom on earth, Christ will reign, and with His followers will rule an earth restored from the ravages of the Tribulation.

Joy to the World

As I write this, Christmas is approaching. Carols echo through and ring joyfully in churches around the world. When

Isaac Watts wrote "Joy to the World," over 250 years ago, he did not intend for it to be a Christmas song, but music to announce the second coming of Christ and His kingdom rule. Remember some of the words? "Joy to the world! the Lord is come; Let earth receive her king. . . . No more let sins and sorrows grow. . . . He rules the world with truth and grace. . . ." This is a song of the Millennium—one of the most theologically disputed themes in the Bible.

Views on the Millennium

What should we believe about this thousand-year period? Will there be an actual time when believers will live in an earthly kingdom, ruled by Jesus? This whole subject has been controversial among Christians, but it is such an important theme in John's narrative of Revelation that we should know where we stand.

A *premillennialist* believes that Christ will bodily return to earth *before* the thousand-year reign begins. He will establish His kingdom and set up His throne in the rebuilt city of Jerusalem. Many places in the Old Testament refer to His kingdom on earth. When we pray the Lord's prayer, we say, "Thy kingdom come, Thy will be done on earth as it is in heaven. . . ." His will cannot be done on earth until Christ's enemies have been defeated and Satan has been bound.

The kingdom ruled by the coming Messiah from the throne of David has been the abiding hope of the Jews for centuries. Premillennialists believe that God's promises to the descendants of Abraham, Isaac, and Jacob will be kept. He guaranteed that the Jews would return to their land and continue there until eternity. There are many Jews who have not believed in God's way of salvation, but for the believing remnant, He has made an unconditional covenant.

Evangelicals and fundamentalists take Scripture seriously and many take a premillennialist position. The belief that the world will get worse, rather than better, is basic to this view. Do you believe man is becoming more moral and improving the status of this world? If you do, please prove it to me.

Years ago many people believed in the *postmillennial* view. Postmillennialists believe the world will continue to get better as Christians spread the gospel and this will be the age of the Millennium. *After* the thousand years, Christ will then take the believers to heaven and condemn the nonbelievers. In America, this view was popular during the nineteenth and early twentieth centuries. Then along came World War I, the Great Depression, the rise of Hitler, World War II, the power of the Soviet Union, and increasing wars throughout the world; the liberal optimism of man achieving Utopia faded.

Today there is a resurgence of this idea from some Christians who espouse Dominion Theology. One of its exponents says: "We are talking about the transformation of this world. Only when the present world has been transformed by the gospel of salvation and the transforming work of the Holy Spirit, as He works through God's redeemed people, will the world at last be delivered completely from sin, at the final judgment. But first, the kingdoms of this world must be steadily transformed into the kingdom of Christ."[1]

The third view is *amillennialism,* which does not believe there will be a thousand-year reign of peace on earth *either before or after* the return of the Lord. Those who believe this way do not believe in a literal fulfillment of the Old Testament prophecies concerning Israel. In fact, the Rapture is not anticipated, nor the warnings concerning the closing days of the ages taken seriously.

Amillennialists believe the church is the fulfillment of the kingdom and that Christ reigns through believers in peace and righteousness.

I imagine that by this time you have no doubt that I am a premillennialist. But why is a Millennium needed at all? Why don't we jump from here to eternity?

Why Do We Need a Millennium?

The Millennium is needed as a reward for the people of God. "Yes, the Lord God is coming with mighty power; he will rule with awesome strength. See, his reward is with him, to each as he has done" (Isaiah 40:10, TLB).

How else can we respond to the disciple's prayer, "Thy kingdom come," without the literal establishment of that kingdom?

The Millennium is needed to redeem creation. We have been told of the terrible devastation of our planet; now it will be made new and beautiful once more.

Another reason for the Millennium is to reemphasize man's depravity. Sin will actually enter into this ideal earth, which verifies that a sinless world is not created by a perfect environment. "You can take man out of the slums, but you can't take the slums out of the man."

Would you like to know what the Millennium will be like for God's people? The Old Testament prophets have given us pictures of this kingdom that have stirred heaven-bound believers for centuries.

Life in the Millennium

It will be peaceful. This will be the time when the prophecy of Micah about beating swords into plowshares and spears into pruning hooks will come true. The United Nations has displayed this saying over its doors, but that promise will never be fulfilled until Christ returns.

There will be no wars. The newspapers will report only good news. Fear will be a thing of the past as everyone walks the streets freely.

Animals will be so tame that there will be no zoos or wild animal parks. Every wild beast will be loving and docile to humans, as well as to each other.

"'On that day, I will banish the names of the idols from the land, and they will be remembered no more,' declares the Lord Almighty. 'I will remove both the prophets and the spirit of impurity from the land'" (Zechariah 13:2).

No more cults . . . no heresy . . . no astrological forecasts. Everyone will unite in one passion to know God.

It will be a time of prosperity. No more unpaid bills, inflation, taxes, or overextended credit cards. It will also be a time of perpetual health. We will not have aches and pains or need for doctors. Most of all, it will be a time of great personal joy. It will be Christmas morning as a child, water on a parched tongue, music to a troubled soul, a warm fire on a cold day. Pure wonder and delight!

During the thousand-year reign, believers will rule with Christ. John saw thrones and a group of people sitting on them who were given authority to judge. The apostle Paul told the Corinthians that saints would judge the world and even judge angels (1 Corinthians 3:4).

John also saw all the Tribulation saints who had not received the mark of the beast, united with their bodies and reigning with Christ. So the dead in Christ and the believers who were caught up in the Rapture, as well as the Tribulation believers, will be rulers during this time. We are not told how they will rule or over whom they will rule, but perhaps the Lord has some plans for those who receive more crowns at the judgment seat of Christ.

I believe King David will be "vice-regent" to the Lord during the kingdom age (see Jeremiah 30:9; Ezekiel 34:23; Hosea 3:5). It is thrilling to know that he will have a place of such importance in the kingdom.

Satan on Death Row

John saw an angel come down from heaven holding a key to the "Abyss." The angel seized Satan and bound him for a thousand years and threw him into the bottomless pit. He will be locked up and a seal placed on him so that he will not be able to practice his crafty deceptions.

For thousands of years, Satan has seduced nations and people into thinking that they can build a world of peace and love without Christ. Sometimes he has deceived people into thinking that education or money would solve personal problems. But his dirty work is over, for a time. At the end of the thousand years "he must be set free for a short time" (Revelation 20:3).

During the Millennium, believers will continue to populate the earth. However, their offspring, living in an ideal environment with King Jesus as the loving, benevolent ruler, can still rebel against God, and some will.

When Satan is released for a time, he will gather some of his old cohorts, Gog and Magog, the nations that hated Israel, and march on Jerusalem once more. This battle will not last long, for fire will come down from heaven and zap them. Then Satan will have his final place of unrest; he will be thrown "into the lake of burning sulfur, where the beast and the false prophet had been thrown. They will be tormented day and night for ever and ever" (Revelation 20:10).

Many times we question why God allows some things to happen. Doesn't it seem strange that once Satan was bound and gagged God would allow him to come back and stir up trouble again? Apparently Satan is released at the end of the Millennium to reveal that even under the ideal conditions of the kingdom, human hearts do not change. Scripture is accurate when it describes the heart as "desperately wicked." The fact that Satan is loosed at the end of the thousand years and some people will still follow him proves how depraved man can be.

Meaning of the First and Second Resurrection

To understand the citizen population of the Millennium, we need to examine the meaning of the resurrections.

Almost 2,000 years ago, Jesus was raised from the dead. Since that time, whenever a believer dies, his soul and spirit go immediately to heaven to be with Jesus. It doesn't make any difference where his body goes, whether it is entombed in an elaborate mausoleum, cremated, buried at sea, or never found. At the Rapture, when Jesus returns in the clouds for His own, the believer's body will be reunited with his soul and spirit in a wonderful, strong, pain-free form.

Seven years later, at the end of the Tribulation, the martyred saints of the Tribulation and the Old Testament saints will be raised from the dead (see Daniel 12:1, 2; Isaiah 26:19). This is the first resurrection. Sometimes it is referred to as the "resurrection unto life." When Jesus comes back to set His feet upon the Mount of Olives to reign during the Millennium, there will not be one body of a believer, from the time of Adam until that time, still in the grave.

The second resurrection is not such a pleasant story. In Revelation 20 it is mentioned: "The rest of the dead did not come to life until the thousand years were ended. . . . And I saw the dead, great and small, standing before the throne, and the books were opened. Another book was opened, which is the book of life. The dead were judged according to what they had done as recorded in the books" (Revelation 20:5, 12–13).

This resurrection takes place one thousand and seven years after the first resurrection. This is when the unsaved dead from Adam until the end of the Millennium are raised and their tormented souls are united with their bodies. The souls and spirits of the unbelievers have been having some agonizing times until now, but at this stage they will appear before the final Judge at the Great White Throne.

The Last Judgment

I once received a ticket for driving in the carpool lane when I was alone in the car. I decided to go to court, instead of paying the fine. That was a dumb thing to do. I was dressed in my Sunday clothes, and I think I arrived on the day all the drunks were there. My one courtroom appearance was not the most pleasant. I should have paid the fine in the first place.

The Great White Throne Judgment will not be like any courtroom experience anyone has ever had. There will be a Judge, but no jury; a Prosecutor, but no defender; a sentence, but no appeal. This is the final judgment of the world.

God is patient, but at that time there will be no more opportunities to accept Him.

John wrote, "Then I saw a great white throne and him who was seated on it. Earth and sky fled from his presence, and there was no place for them" (Revelation 20:11).

Somewhere between heaven and earth this judgment will take place. Jesus Christ Himself will conduct the trial, and no one is better qualified. He did all He could to save man. Since man has rejected Him, he must be judged by Him.

All the unsaved dead will be standing there, the great and the small from the ranks in the church and in the world. The biggest and the most famous down to the least and unknown will go before that awesome and majestic throne.

The purpose of the Great White Throne Judgment is not to determine if a person is saved. All who will be saved will have been saved by this time. This is a judgment on the evil works of the unsaved. Men are not sent to hell because of being murderers or liars, they are sent to hell because they are unrighteous.

John tells us that men are judged out of the book of life and out of the book of works. Although we are not told specifically, I believe there are at least five books that will be opened on that fateful day.

First, the *Book of Conscience*. Undoubtedly there will be some standing there who will say, "I never heard about God's law or the way of salvation . . . how can I be found guilty?" The apostle Paul wrote to the early church: ". . . since they show that the requirements of the law are written on their hearts, their consciences also bearing witness, and their thoughts now accusing, now even defending them" (Romans 2:15).

In other words, man will be condemned because he violated his conscience during his life upon the earth.

Second, the *Book of Words* that Jesus explained, "For by your words you will be acquitted, and by your words you will be condemned" (Matthew 12:37).

Those words might be, "I'm not interested in spiritual things." Or, "Sure, I believe in God, but everybody has his own god he worships."

Third, the *Book of Secret Words.* "This will take place on the day when God will judge men's secrets through Jesus Christ" (Romans 2:16).

D. L. Moody, the famous evangelist, used to say that if a man ever invented a camera that could take a photograph of the human heart, he would starve to death, for people would refuse to have this revealing picture exposed.

Fourth, there's the *Book of Public Works.* ". . . he will reward each person according to what he has done" (Matthew 16:27).

It is dreadful to think of what the sentences will be for some infamous people.

Finally, the last one is the *Book of Life.* "If anyone's name was not written in the book of life, he was thrown into the lake of fire" (Revelation 20:15).

This book is an amazing record. It will contain the name of every single person born into the world. If, by the time a person dies, he has not received God's provision of sacrifice to remove his sin, his name will be blotted out of the pages.

The scene at the judgment seat will be heartrending. As each person steps forward, God will open the various books, pointing out what was required to have been accepted as a child of God. When He solemnly opens the Book of Life and begins to look down this immense directory for the person's name, His gentle hands will turn the pages, wishing to find the name of the accused. But it won't be there.

He will say sadly, and with great reluctance, "Depart from me, you who are cursed, into the eternal fire prepared for the devil and his angels" (Matthew 25:41).

As the person trembles, frantically trying to defend himself, the Lord slowly shakes His head and says the saddest words anyone could ever hear: "I never knew you . . . I never knew you."

The condemned will die a second time. From the second death there is no resurrection. These people will wander through the darkness of eternity, the black night that never ends, as derelicts of humanity.

I don't enjoy writing about this scene. Even though Jesus Christ spoke frequently of hell, today we have made it so common that we have no fear. Without fear, there is no compassion.

I remember the words of a song that used to be sung in gospel meetings and revivals when I was a boy. My dad was a preacher, and I can still feel the chill that would go through me when I heard a message on the Great White Throne Judgment. I did not want to be there.

> I dreamed that the great judgment morning
> Had dawned, and the trumpet had blown;
> I dreamed that the nations had gathered
> To judgment before the white throne;
>
> From the throne came a bright, shining angel
> And stood by the land and the sea,
> And swore with his hand raised to heaven,
> That time was no longer to be.
>
> The rich man was there but his money
> Had melted and vanished away;
> A pauper he stood in the judgment,
> His debts were too heavy to pay;
>
> The great man was there, but his greatness
> When death came, was left far behind!
> The angel that opened the records,
> Not a trace of his greatness could find.

The gambler was there and the drunkard,
And the man that had sold them the drink,
With the people who sold them the license
Together in hell they did sink.

The moral man came to the judgment,
But his self-righteous rags would not do;
The men who had crucified Jesus
Had passed off as moral men, too.

The soul that had put off salvation—
"Not tonight; I'll get saved by and by;
No time now to think of religion!"
At last, he had found time to die.

And oh, what a weeping and wailing,
As the lost were told of their fate;
They cried for the rocks and the mountains,
They prayed, but their prayer was too late.[2]

Thank God we are not too late. We can become the citizens of a new heaven and a new earth for all eternity.

19

PARADISE
REGAINED

We have traveled with John on a prophetic time machine, and as we look back at the people we've met and the places we've seen, we could title our trip *An Incredible Journey.*

Now we've reached the end of our journey and will be given a preview of eternity future; a new heaven and a new earth will be created. Although it's difficult to imagine anything more wonderful than the heaven we inhabit upon our deaths, the eternal heaven will be even more glorious. The crowning jewel in paradise will be the Holy City, the New Jerusalem.

Entrance to a New Heaven and a New Earth

John had viewed so much tragedy and triumph that it must have been overwhelming to see his vision end in such blazing color. He wrote:

"Then I saw a new heaven and a new earth, for the first heaven and the first earth had passed away, and there was no longer any sea. . . . He who was seated on the throne said, 'I am making everything new!' Then he said, 'Write this down, for these words are trustworthy and true'" (Revelation 21:1, 5).

It seems strange that the New Heaven and the New Earth will be without seas. Since three-fourths of the globe today is under water, this new world will certainly be different. We know that oceans separate people, so perhaps the reason there will be no large bodies of water is so we may have one unified continent. John had known the loneliness of isolation on the Island of Patmos, separated by the Aegean Sea from his friends and church ministry on the mainland.

The New Earth will be filled with righteousness (2 Peter 3:13). There will be nothing to mar our perfect relationship with Jesus and with each other. The thoughts and deeds that dominate our existence on Planet Earth will be gone—no jealousy, anger, cheating, murder, fornication, dirt, slums, or pollution. If we think that sounds bland, wait until we discover what *will* be there.

Will we miss our "old life"? Not at all. The prophet Isaiah wrote: "Behold, I will create new heavens and a new earth. The former things will not be remembered, nor will they come to mind" (65:17).

There will be no death and no mourning. The heaven sung about in love songs or painted by Renaissance artists is just a microcosm of what the real thing will be. The Lord who created this beautiful earth we possess today has some real surprises for us, I'm sure.

What Will Happen to the Old Heaven and Earth?

Here's a description of the end of this present world that was given to the apostle Peter. He said:

"But the day of the Lord will come like a thief. The heavens will disappear with a roar; the elements will be destroyed by fire, and the earth and everything in it will be laid bare. . . . That day will bring about the destruction of the heavens by fire, and the elements will melt in the heat" (2 Peter 3:10, 12).

I believe that Peter's words do not convey a total annihilation of the old earth and heaven, but rather a remaking of them.

In both the Old and New Testaments, the words for "new" mean freshness or a renovation. It's like taking an old building and remodeling it. One scholar said this:

"The newness of the heaven and of the earth shall be like our own. We shall be the same persons and have the same body and the same soul that we now have; but these made entirely new. . . . The same shall be true with regard to the new heaven and the new earth."[1]

Revelation reveals only what we should know for now. There are some mysteries that God will leave for us to discover when we arrive in Paradise; this must be why we have so few descriptions of our eternal home. He has described, however, the New Jerusalem, the center of the new universe and the capital from which Jesus will rule.

The New Jerusalem: How Big?

The longing for a future glorious city of God can be traced back as far as the Old Testament patriarchs. Abraham ". . . was looking forward to the city with foundations, whose architect and builder is God" (Hebrews 11:10).

Paul mentioned this city in his letter to the Galatians. He called it "the Jerusalem which is above" (Galatians 4:26).

The "New Jerusalem" (Revelation 21:2; 3:12) is just one of the several names given to this future city of God. It is also called The Holy City, the Heavenly Jerusalem, and Mount Zion. Whatever it is named, it will be a holy and beautiful place, more perfect than the Garden of Eden.

John wrote: "The angel who talked with me had a measuring rod of gold to measure the city, its gates and its walls. The city was laid out like a square, as long as it was wide. He measured the city with the rod and found it to be 12,000 stadia in length, and as wide and high as it is long" (Revelation 21:15, 16).

I cannot comprehend the size of this city, but I accept the Word of God by faith. Since the Bible is a supernatural book, we should expect to discover within it supernatural truth. All the cities in the world are mere villages compared to the New Jerusalem. One person calculated the total base area of the city would be 1,750,329 square miles. (And this is not counting its height, which reaches far above the atmosphere into the regions of space!)

John Walvoord said: "Whatever its shape, a city of large dimensions would be proper, if it is to be the residence of the saved of all ages including infants who died before reaching the age of accountability. It is not necessarily true, however, to hold that everyone will live continually within its walls throughout eternity. The implications are that there is plenty of room for everyone and this city provides a residence for the saints of all ages."[2]

Description of the City

Can you imagine a holy city? It would be a community where no one lied, no shady business deals were ever discussed, no unclean movies or pictures were seen. The New Jerusalem will be holy because everyone in it will be holy. Whatever discouraging or dark thoughts enter our minds today will be erased.

Let's take a walk with John through one of the twelve gates where we may enter the city. We see a 250-foot wall made of jasper, a clear, unblemished crystal. No city has ever had such a magnificent enclosure. Perhaps we will see a population sign outside, with so many zeros at the end we cannot comprehend it. Our minds cannot grasp how much a billion is, let alone multiple trillions.

As we continue through one of the gates of pearl, we are overcome with awe. Perhaps the apostle Peter is standing at the gate, perhaps not. No one is going to question our entrance, however, contrary to all the myths which surround the "pearly gates."

By the way, the gates are not just encrusted with pearls, they *are* pearl. Some scholars stumble at the thought of such a gigantic gem and say the description is merely figurative. However, the Bible says they are solid pearl, so why should we doubt it?

On every gate of the city is the name of one of the twelve tribes of Israel. The gates are a part of the wall that surrounds the city like a glittering bracelet.

The foundations of the city walls are "decorated with every kind of precious stone" (Revelation 21:19).

We count twelve precious stones, varying in color and brilliance, melding together in a vivid display atop the jasper foundation. These stones may be classified into the four basic colors that every artist uses in variation on his palette. This time it is the Master Architect who has drawn the blueprints and specified the most exquisite colors. Imagine twelve of the most precious stones Tiffany's might display, layered on top of each other and blending together in a fireworks display of splendor. On the twelve foundations the names of the twelve apostles are inscribed. However, the beauty of the city from the outside will only be a taste of what is inside.

As we pass the foundations and enter the city, we are so grateful for the wonderful plan that made it possible for us to be there.

". . . and the city of pure gold, as pure as glass. . . . The street of the city was of pure gold, like transparent glass" (Revelation 21:18, 21).

If you've looked at pure gold, you know that it is not transparent, but opaque. But the gold of heaven is unbelievable—we are able to look right through its clear depths as we walk on it.

There will be no temple in the New Jerusalem, because there will be no need for it. The Lord Himself will be the temple.

Surrounding us is a light that is strong enough for us to see our way, but not so blinding that it impairs our vision. We are puzzled about where the light is coming from, because there is no sun and no moon. John assures us, "The city does not need the sun or the moon to shine on it, for the glory of God gives it light, and the Lamb is its lamp" (Revelation 21:23).

Our angel guide has more to show John and us. We see a river of life flowing down through the middle of the city, and an immense tree spanning the river. This magnificent tree is laden with fruit and we are told there is a different crop every month. This will be the ultimate fruit-of-the-month gift package.

More than one believer has asked the question, "Will we eat in heaven?" It's almost as if the true joy of eternity is at stake if we are not able to sit down to a heavenly banquet.

When the angels were entertained by Abraham, they ate. After Jesus was raised from the dead, He ate. At the Lord's Supper, Jesus said that He would not drink the fruit of the vine until that day when He would drink it new with us in the kingdom of our Father (Matthew 26:29). We are going to be at the marriage supper of the Lamb. And, of course, we're going to eat the twelve different kinds of fruit on those trees of paradise. We shall certainly eat in heaven and not be concerned about gaining a pound.

Nothing we have seen, though, will compare with our approach to the throne of God when we shall see His face.

"The angel said to me, 'These words are trustworthy and true. The Lord, the God of the spirits of the prophets, sent his angel to show his servants the things that must soon take place'" (Revelation 22:6).

Only the citizens whose names are written in the Lamb's Book of Life will take this walk.

Missing in Heaven

Jesus is preparing the New Jerusalem for us now. It will be "prepared as a bride beautifully dressed for her husband"

(Revelation 21:2). Our mansions are built, furnished, and waiting for occupancy. There's not a Beverly Hills 30,000-square-foot extravaganza that can compare with what the Master Builder has designed for His family.

Paradise has some missing elements, because God has deliberately omitted certain familiar aspects of earthly life.

First, there will be no churches or sanctuaries. This means I will be out of a job, but I won't mind a bit. Why would there be need for a church, when our cause to worship is present with us?

We will not see the sun, but there will be no cloudy days. His light will be among us forevermore.

In our eternal home there will be no sadness, no more tears. "He will wipe every tear from their eyes" (Revelation 21:4). This has been puzzling, for we are now viewing eternity, and why would there be tears in anyone's eyes? Perhaps there will be tears because we have stood at the judgment seat of Christ and remembered lost opportunities to tell someone about Him. Perhaps we will have shed tears over the agony of the lost during the Tribulation. Whatever may have been the reason before, we will never experience sorrow in the New Jerusalem.

We will never be separated from our loved ones. There will be no painful farewells, just a prolonged love story. No arguments, no hurt feelings, no injured egos.

Doctors and dentists will also be out of work, for there will be no sickness and no pain. People who have been confined to wheel chairs will be able to run; the blind will see unmarred beauty; the deaf will hear the heavenly choirs; the wounded will be whole.

We will know each other, for we will have glorified bodies, just as Jesus has. For all eternity He will be with us and we will know and see Him. We know this is true, because He has told us: "And I heard a loud voice from the throne saying, 'Now the dwelling of God is with men, and he will live with them. They will be his people, and God himself will be with them and be their God'" (Revelation 21:3).

Today people cry out, "O, God, where are You?" But in that day they will know.

What Will We Do in Heaven?

We will sing in heaven. If you mumble the words to songs on earth, you will have a voice like an angel in heaven. (Where do you think that phrase came from?) God will give us perfect instruments to play to accompany the choirs of thousands—or perhaps millions. We cannot comprehend how glorious this music will be.

We will serve God in heaven. We will function in the true sense as servants of God. There are many things we would have liked to have done on earth, but didn't have the time nor the talent, but when we are citizens of the eternal heaven, we will fulfill all our desires. Our service will be according to our tastes and our ability. We will do tasks happily, without weariness. Many people hate what they're doing on earth—they don't like their jobs, their bosses, the places in which they work. But our service in heaven will be just the opposite. We'll love every eternal minute of it.

We will share endless times of fellowship with others. Imagine a time when we can meet the great people of past generations, those we never could have met on earth, but now we can spend quality time with them. There will be no generation gap. I want to meet John and Paul and Peter. How wonderful it will be to talk with Daniel and David and Joseph. In eternity, every single person will be important.

As we grow older, and more and more of our loved ones are in heaven, we long for the time we will see them again. How wonderful it will be to talk with the parents, children, relatives, and friends we have lost for a time during our earthly life. If someone near and dear to you has died, each day you live brings you closer to seeing him again. The years of loneliness without those we love will be erased. We will have forever to love and be loved.

We will talk with Jesus—not in the way we talk to Him today, in our prayers and quiet times, but face to face, asking questions and getting answers. Can you imagine asking Him all the questions we have wanted to have answered on earth?

Tell Me about Heaven . . . *Much Later*

We may want to go to heaven some day, but we may think, *Let that "some day" be when I'm very, very old and have done everything on earth I want to do.*

I can understand those thoughts. When my wife, Donna, and I were engaged, there was a conference on the campus of the college we were attending, and the preacher spoke on the second coming of Christ and on heaven. This was in the spring and we were to be married that June. When I took Donna home to the dorm that night, she said, "David, I hope you don't think I'm unspiritual, and I really want the Lord to come, but not until after June 29."

Many of us feel the way Donna did. *Come, Lord, but not now!* But as we move through life, we become more realistic about the future. If we get heaven straightened out in our minds, the most important thing we can do is to take as many people with us as we can.

I heard the story of a mother who was dying in one of our Eastern cities a few years ago. She had a family of many children, and she knew the burden of raising this family would be very difficult for her husband.

Before her death, each of the children was brought to her, one at a time, to say good-bye. From the oldest to youngest, they came into the room and kissed her as she told them how much she loved them and blessed each one. At last the baby was placed in her arms, and as she pressed him to her heart, the nurse knew it was not long until she would die. Gently she took the child from the mother's arms. With her last words, the woman whispered to her husband, "My darling, please bring these children home with you when you come."

That puts it all together. As parents, as teachers, as believers in Jesus Christ, from the first day they can remember, tell the children about Jesus, and how they can come to Him.

We are responsible to bring our children home when we go to live in Paradise forever.

20

THE TIME
IS NEAR

John has seen it all—he has recorded the final scenes of a new heaven and earth, and now he writes the epilogue to the book of Revelation. We are reminded again that what God starts, He finishes. There are no loose ends in His plan for the universe.

In the prologue, we were told that prophecy is from God: "The revelation of Jesus Christ, which God gave him . . ." (1:1). We also know that He sent an angel to bring this to John, who was the human agent for these amazing messages. When we read or hear this prophecy, we are promised a blessing. We are also told in the opening scenes that "the time is near."

As we read the epilogue in Revelation 22, the same promises are repeated (22:6, 7, 8).

God doesn't change His mind part way through a book, like some novelists do, and decide to end His story with a question mark. What He begins, He finishes.

But what should we do with what we have learned? Some people get on a prophetic kick and take every daily happening or world headline and relate it to a specific prophecy. The prophetic word will determine the events of the world—not the events determine the truth of prophecy. However, I do see many events today happening so rapidly that God's prophecies are unrolling faster than we thought could happen even a year ago.

This is not a time to be a prophecy-buff without understanding what God's will is for us right now.

Our Responsibility

"These words are trustworthy and true" (Revelation 22:6).

Our responsibility is to be obedient to the truth. No book in the Bible has been attacked more than Revelation. Along with Daniel, Isaiah, and other prophets, it is ignored or ridiculed. God says not to fool with it, add to it, or leave anything out. He warns: ". . . everyone who hears the words of the prophecy of this book: If anyone adds anything to them, God will add to him the plagues described in this book. And if anyone takes words away from this book of prophecy, God will take away from him his share in the tree of life and in the holy city" (22:18).

I believe this applies to those who do not bother to teach from the book of Revelation. One minister said to me, "I want to teach what is relevant to everyday life, and I just can't see any relevancy in Revelation."

Every book in the Bible is relevant. "Every word of God is flawless. . . . Do not add to his words, or he will rebuke you and prove you a liar" (Proverbs 30:5, 6).

Every liberal preacher should read those words. When someone adds to the Scripture what is not there, or takes away what *is* there, God has some strong things to say.

It costs something to believe in what the Bible says, especially when you begin to talk about the prophecies of things to come. We may be treated like we have the plague, but the price we pay is worth it.

Until Jesus comes again, we need to walk submissively, obeying Him and the truth He has given us. His last will and testament urges us to read it, follow it, believe it, and study it.

Until He comes, I want to worship Him. This is what John did. He was an emotional person, perhaps even a sentimentalist; remember John was called the "Beloved Apostle." Several times in Revelation, he came unglued and simply passed out when he saw something too awesome for him. He had a habit of confusing the messenger for the one who sent the message. It was then that he was told, "Worship God!"(22:9).

What do we say when we worship God? Many places in Revelation we are given the guidelines for worship.

"Holy, holy, holy is the Lord God Almighty, who was, and is, and is to come" (4:8).

"You are worthy, our Lord and God, to receive glory and honor and power, for you created all things, and by your will they were created and have their being" (4:11).

"Salvation belongs to our God, who sits on the throne, and to the Lamb. . . . Amen! Praise and glory and wisdom and thanks and honor and power and strength be to our God for ever and ever. Amen!" (7:10, 12).

I don't think the evangelical church as a whole comes even close to worshiping God. That's what we are going to do throughout eternity, so we better begin to practice.

Prophecy is the force behind witnessing. If we can study Revelation and understand the Tribulation, but remain indifferent, then we have not grasped what this is all about.

Prophecy is not given to us to understand and then become drop-outs, believing Jesus is coming soon and goals are not important. That is not true at all. We are told to work even more fervently if we believe He is coming soon. "Behold, I am coming soon! My reward is with me, and I will give to everyone according to what he has done" (22:12).

Remember, at the judgment seat of Christ we are going to give account of what we have done for the Lord while we were living on earth.

There are some good Christians who say we shouldn't work for rewards, but I believe our work is to be a labor of love for Him, and as such we will reap the rewards.

Robert Murray McCheyne was a great man of God, and he lived only thirty years. However, he accomplished more for the Lord in his short life than most of us do. He had a watch which had inscribed on it: "The night cometh." Jesus said, "Night is coming, when no one can work" (John 9:4).

The days, the weeks, the years pass so quickly. Now is the time to work, for there will come a time when it's too late.

We are told to watch expectantly for His return. He has said, "Behold, I am coming soon!" (22:7). In Revelation Jesus tells us the same thing four times. He wants to make sure we remember His message to us.

The story was told of a girl whose fiancé sailed off to the Holy Land. He told her he would return to take her as his bride. Every night she went down to the shore and lit a fire as a sign in the night for the ship she was waiting for.

This is the way we should be, waiting on the shore for our lover to return.

I Am Coming Soon

Two invitations are given in this final testament. "The Spirit and the bride say, 'Come!' And let him who hears say, 'Come!' Whoever is thirsty, let him come; and whoever wishes, let him take the free gift of the water of life" (22:17).

One invitation is for Christ to come back to the world, the other is for the world to come back to Christ.

Why do people come to Christ? It's because they are thirsty. Something is lacking in their lives; they are parched because everything else seems so dry and empty. It's not a coincidence that the Bible calls Christians the salt of the world.

My uncle had a farm, and I remember asking him one time why he had those big chunks of salt where the cattle could lick them. He said it was because they needed to get thirsty and hungry enough to eat nutritious food.

A person does not come to Christ by his intellect alone—or even with his heart alone. He comes to Christ because he decides to do so. It is a matter of the will—whosoever *will* let him come.

What is the requirement for salvation? It's so simple—just take the free gift that is offered. We don't have to work for it or give up anything for it, we just need to decide to take it.

God's desire is for us to accept the gift of Jesus Christ, who died on the cross that we might be saved and have eternal life in the New Heaven and the New Earth.

When He puts His final signature on His will we have just opened and read, He says:

YES, I AM COMING SOON.

NOTES

Chapter 1

1. "On the Mountain's Brink," U.S. Dept. of Agriculture booklet, 25.
2. Rowe Findley, "St. Helens: Mountain with a Death Wish," *National Geographic,* January 1981, 20.
3. See Isaiah 7:14; Genesis 14:10; Jeremiah 23:5; Micah 5:12; Psalm 110:1.
4. See Deuteronomy 18:18; Isaiah 33:22; Psalm 2:6; Isaiah 42:1; Isaiah 6:1, 2.

Chapter 2

1. George Church, "Freedom," *Time,* 20 November 1989, 29.
2. W. Graham Scroggie, *The Great Unveiling* (Grand Rapids: Zondervan, 1979), 43.
3. Louis Talbot, *The Revelation of Jesus Christ* (Grand Rapids: Eerdmans, 1937), 15.
4. Vernard Eiler, *The Most Revealing Book of the Bible — Making Sense out of Revelation* (Grand Rapids: Eerdmans, 1974), 48.
5. See Matthew 24:30; Exodus 19:9; Exodus 30:34; Matthew 17:5; Acts 1:9; Daniel 7:13.
6. *Time,* 15 August 1988, 40.
7. Quoted in H. L. Mencken, *The New Dictionary of Quotations* (New York: Alfred A. Knopf, 1966), 1266.

Chapter 3

1. Aleksandr Solzhenitsyn, *The Gulag Archipelago* (New York: Harper & Row, 1973), 3.
2. See John 16:33 and 21:20.
3. See Isaiah 2:12; Zechariah 14:1, 4; Zephaniah 1:7, 8.
4. See Genesis 18:1, 2; Exodus 3:6; Numbers 22:31; Isaiah 6:5; Matthew 17:6; Acts 9:1–6.
5. Told in *Guideposts,* November 1988, 10.
6. Billy Graham, *Facing Death and the Life After* (Waco, TX: Word, Inc., 1987), 119.

Chapter 4

1. Charles Haddon Spurgeon Sermon Notes.
2. Marcus L. Loane, *They Overcame* (Grand Rapids: Eerdmans, 1937), 41.

3. Corrie ten Boom, *Marching Orders for the End Times* (London: Christian Literature Crusade, 1969), 83, 86.

4. Sergui Grossu, *The Church in Today's Catacombs* (New Rochelle, NY: Arlington House Publishers, 1975), 57.

5. Account taken from *Eerdmans Handbook to the History of Christianity* (Berkhamsted, Herts, England: Lion Publishing, 1977), 81.

6. J. A. Seiss, *The Apocalypse, Lectures on the Book of Revelation* (Grand Rapids: Zondervan, 1964).

7. John R. W. Stott, *What Christ Thinks of the Church* (Grand Rapids: Eerdmans, 1958), 72.

8. Ibid., 88.

9. *Los Angeles Times,* Part II, 4 March 1989, 7.

Chapter 5

1. Brian Lanker, "The Meaning of Life," *Life,* December 1988.

2. Gary North, *Liberating Planet Earth* (Fort Worth, TX: Dominion Press, 1987), 9.

3. Richard Halverson, quoted in *The Omega Letter* (North Bay, Ontario, Canada, February 1989), 4.

4. John Stott, *What Christ Thinks of the Church,* 116.

5. David Wilkerson, "The Laodicean Lie!" *Evangelist* magazine, December 1986, 15–17.

6. G. Campbell Morgan, *The Letters of Our Lord* (Old Tappan, NJ: Fleming H. Revell), 108

Chapter 6

1. *Los Angeles Times,* Part V, 15 August 1988, 1.

2. *Los Angeles Times,* Part V, 1 May 1989, 1.

3. Douglas R. Groothuis, *Unmasking the New Age* (Downers Grove, IL: Intervarsity Press, 1989), 25.

4. Ibid., 28, 29.

5. Edward C. Wolf, "Avoiding a Mass Extinction of the Species," *State of the World* (New York: W. W. Norton & Co., 1988), 114.

6. Ibid., 101.

7. *Time,* 2 January 1989, 48.

8. Lester Brown and Edward Wolf, "Reclaiming the Future," *State of the World,* 178, 170.

9. Ibid., 171.

10. Harvey Fineberg, "The Social Dimensions of AIDS," *Scientific American,* October 1988, 128.

11. Ibid.
12. *Life,* February 1989, 40.
13. *Science,* October 1987, 270.
14. *Time,* 8 May 1989, 20.
15. *The Christian World Report,* February 1989, 9.
16. "The Future and You," *Life,* February 1989, 53.
17. *State of the World,* 18.
18. Ibid., 170.
19. Advertisement, *Time,* 13 March 1989.
20. *Time,* 2 January 1989, 30.
21. Ibid.

Chapter 7
1. Quoted in Stephen Covey, *The Seven Habits of Highly Effective People* (New York: Simon & Schuster, Inc., 1989), 115.

Chapter 8
1. Donald Grey Barnhouse, *Revelation: An Expository Commentary* (Grand Rapids: Zondervan, 1967), 122.
2. Allan Bloom, *The Closing of the American Mind* (New York: Simon & Schuster, 1987), 61.
3. Ibid.
4. "Top Official and Expert Urge More AIDS Funds," *New York Times,* 27 September 1985.
5. J. W. Curran, "The Epidemiology and Prevention of the Acquired Immunodeficiency Syndrome," *Annual of Internal Medicine* (1985), 657–662.
6. *Encyclopedia Americana,* Vol. 23, p. 264.

Chapter 9
1. Jacob Presser, *The Destruction of the Dutch Jews* (New York: Dutton, 1969), 336.
2. Henry Morris, *The Revelation Record* (Wheaton, IL: Tyndale House, 1983), 119.
3. W. A. Criswell, *Expository Sermons on Revelation* (Grand Rapids: Zondervan, 1962), 106–107.
4. John Walvoord, *The Revelation of Jesus Christ* (Chicago: Moody Press, 1966), 99.
5. *Time,* 30 October 1989, 44.

Chapter 10
1. J. A. Seiss, *The Apocalypse* (Grand Rapids: Zondervan, 1964), 161.

2. Charles Colson, *Born Again* (Old Tappan, NJ: Chosen Books, 1976), 115.

3. Ibid., 130.

Chapter 11

1. H. A. Ironside, *Lectures on the Revelation of Jesus Christ* (New York: Loizeaux Brothers, 1920), 157.

2. Walter Scott, *Exposition of the Revelation of Jesus Christ* (London: Pickering and Inglis, Ltd.), 203.

3. *Time,* 29 January 1990, 57.

4. Henry Morris, *The Revelation Record,* 174.

5. Vance Havner, "Prophetic Doctrine and Practical Duty," *Moody Monthly,* July 1940.

Chapter 12

1. Walter Scott, *Exposition of the Revelation of Jesus Christ,* 223–224.

2. Jerry M. Landay, *Dome of the Rock,* Newsweek, 1972, 43.

3. *Biblical Archeology Review,* March/April, 1983.

4. Warren Wiersbe, *Be Victorious* (Wheaton, IL: Victor Books, 1985), 94.

Chapter 13

1. Douglas MacArthur, *Reminiscences* (New York: McGraw Hill, 1964), 109.

2. Merrill Unger, *Biblical Demonology* (Wheaton, IL: VanKampen Press, 1952), 197.

3. Paul E. Billheimer, *Destined to Overcome—The Technique of Spiritual Warfare* (Minneapolis: Bethany House Publishers, 1982), 31–33.

Chapter 14

1. Scott Sullivan, "Who's Afraid of 1992?" *Newsweek,* 31 October 1988, 34.

2. John Naisbitt and Patrica Aburdene, *Megatrends 2000* (New York: William Morrow & Co., Inc., 1990), 61.

3. Ibid., 271.

4. *McCall's,* March 1989, 69.

Chapter 15

1. H. A. Ironside, *Lectures on the Book of Revelation.*

2. John Walvoord, *The Revelation of Jesus Christ,* 244.

3. Francis Schaeffer, *The Church Before the Watching World* (Downers Grove, IL: Intervarsity Press, 1971), 79.

4. Naisbitt, *Megatrends 2000,* 293.

5. Ibid., 294.

6. Joseph Carr, *The Lucifer Connection* (Lafayette, LA: Huntington House, Inc., 1987), 15, 16.

7. See *Halley's Bible Handbook* (Grand Rapids: Zondervan, 1965), 777.

8. See J. A. Seiss, *The Apocalypse: Lectures on the Book of Revelation* (Grand Rapids: Zondervan, 1967), 467.

9. *Encylopedia Americana* (1988 Annual), 291.

Chapter 16

1. J. Vernon McGee, *Through the Bible with J. Vernon McGee* (Pasadena, CA: Through the Bible Radio, 1983), 1022.

2. Henry Morris, *The Revelation Record,* 61–62.

3. Lester Brown and Christopher Flavin, "The Earth's Vital Signs," *State of the World,* 3.

Chapter 17

1. William Culbertson and Herman B. Centz, eds., *Understanding the Times* (Grand Rapids: Zondervan, 1956), 174.

2. Kenneth Woodward, "Heaven," *Newsweek,* 27 March 1989, 54.

3. Ibid.

4. Ibid.

Chapter 18

1. Gary North, *Liberating Planet Earth* (Ft. Worth, TX: Dominion Press, 1987), 8, 9.

2. *Rodeheaver's Gospel Solos and Duets* (Winona Lake, IN: The Rodeheaver Hall-Mack Co., 1925).

Chapter 19

1. R. C. H. Lenski, *The Interpretation of St. John's Revelation* (Columbus, OH: Luther Book Concern, 1942), 614, 615,

2. John Walvoord, *The Revelation of Jesus Christ,* 95.